HOW TO TEACH TECHNICIANS
(without putting them to sleep!)

2nd Edition

By: Dan Holohan

© 2018 by HeatingHelp.com

All rights reserved. No part of this publication may be reproduced or used in any form or by any means – graphic, electronic, or mechanical, including photocopying, recording, taping, or information storage and retrieval systems – without written permission of the publisher. So there!

In loving memory of Dave Nelsen
1952-1998

*"A teacher affects eternity;
no one can tell where his influence stops."*

- Henry Adams

A note on gender

In the interest of smoother prose I'm using the masculine gender throughout this book. I'm well aware that there are *many* fine female technicians and teachers working today, and I respect you all.

Dan Holohan

Contents

Prologue: Beer cans and other considerations 9

1. We all have to start someplace, eh? 19
2. The greatest fear of all 47
3. Logistics 81
4. Let me hear your body talk 97
5. How to tell a story 119
6. The power of fun 145
7. Tool time 165
8. The "Seminar in a Box" 189
9. Facing challenges 213
10. The meeting place 235
11. Happy endings 257

Revisiting all that I once believed

I wrote this book in 1999 at the urging of Dave Nelsen, a friend who died much too soon from spinal meningitis. Dave was a service manager for a Long Island, NY oil-heating company. He also taught classes for the National Association of Oil-Heating Service Managers. Dave thought he had the flu and kept going to work rather than to the doctor. That decision killed him.

I had been teaching the same technicians as Dave was teaching, but also many more because my work as a writer took me all over America. At the time of this writing, I had taught about 40,000 technicians. Dave and I would swap stories and one day he asked me to write it all down. So I did.

When I finished my speaking career in 2016, that number had risen to more than 200,000. It was quite a journey, and I learned a lot along the way.

The first version of this book, for instance, had me railing against this new thing called PowerPoint, which was just 12 years old at the time. I couldn't stand the way most people used PowerPoint for listing bullet points, and I was very happy with the nonlinear nature of my overhead projector and slides back then. I didn't have to follow a particular order with the overhead slides, and that made me able to answer any question that came up, no matter where it was in the presentation.

I came around to PowerPoint, though, but not before figuring out how to best use it when teaching technicians. I'll tell you about that in these pages.

I also rethought much of what I believed in 1999 about teaching. Those thoughts are all here as well and I hope they help you be an even better teacher of the people who work with their hands as well as their heads.

And to all the techs I taught, thanks for teaching *me*.

Dan Holohan

Summer, 2017

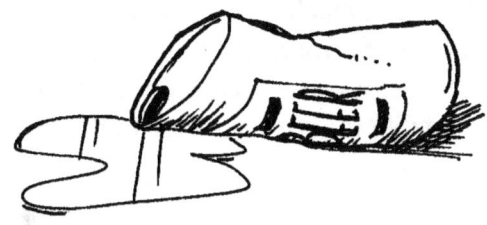

PROLOGUE
Beer cans and other considerations

The four-legged stool

I once had a technician throw an empty beer can at me. I was pretty young and quite dumb at the time. I deserved it, and I'll get around to telling you that tale in a little while. For now, though, I just needed to mention the business with the beer can because that was one of my motivations for wanting to write all of this stuff down.

To keep you from getting hit by an empty beer can.

Or pizza crust.

Or worse!

You see, how you decide to teach these technicians is going to affect not only *them*, but also *you*.

And not only you, but also your day-to-day business if they happen to be working for you. Technicians are the people that your customers see most often. Their attitude and their performance will reflect upon *you* as a businessperson. They can make you or break you.

If you're teaching technicians that work for other people, your efforts will have just as much impact on *their* businesses. As a teacher, you're both responsible *and* accountable for what you say to the technicians, and *how* you say it.

And that's why it's in *everyone's* best interest for you to learn how to teach. And you know what? There's a lot more to effective teaching than just standing up in front of a roomful of technicians and talking about a subject you know well. If the technicians are falling asleep they're not going to remember very much of that brilliance you've been spouting. It's not just *what* you say; it's *how* you say it.

Have you ever sat through a boring lecture where the guy up front droned on like an old propeller plane? What did *you* carry away from that experience? Not much, I'll bet.

If *you* choose to teach then *you* have a responsibility to be interesting. You are one leg of what I've always thought of as a four-legged stool. Here are the four legs:

1. You
2. The tools you're using to teach
3. The setting (which includes, but is not limited to, the room you're in, its location on the planet, the comfort level of the room, the lighting, the food, if that's included)
4. The technicians who come to hear what you have to say

You have control over the first three of those "legs." You can change the tools, the setting, and yourself. You can make just about anything that you want of these three things. And what you make of them can have an *enormous* impact on the fourth "leg" of the stool – the technicians, the people you are trying to educate.

On the other hand, you also have to power to make it all fall flat on its face.

That's a pretty big responsibility, don't you think?

Do unto others . . .

So here's what I wish for you. I wish for you to be *successful* as a teacher of technicians. And to get to that point, all I'd like for you to do *right now* is to just think for a moment about how *you* would like to be taught if *you* were sitting out there in that classroom.

I'll bet you'd probably like to get answers to things you've *always* wondered about but didn't know how to ask (or maybe you were afraid to ask). Maybe you've never completely understood, say, the refrigeration cycle. Maybe you're not comfortable with controls. Maybe you can't read a blueprint or an electrical schematic. You know why? You've never been properly taught, and at this point in your life, you're a bit embarrassed about that. Wouldn't it be great if someone just walked up to you and gave you the answers?

And I'll bet you'd like to get those answers in plain English, wouldn't you? I mean, who the heck appreciates mumbo jumbo? You just want to ask a straight question and get an honest answer without being ridiculed for asking, right?

I feel the same way. I always have. So we agree. Good.

Now, what else?

Well, you'd probably also like to have a few laughs while you're getting your answers, wouldn't you? I mean, life should be *fun*, shouldn't it? Why the heck should learning have to hurt? Learning was fun when you were a little kid, wasn't it?

It can be fun again – *if* your teacher is good.

So where do we go from here?

How about the meeting place? You want that place to be comfortable, of course. If you're a big guy, you're not going to learn very much if you're stuck for hours on an uncomfortable chair in a cramped place, are you? Of course not. The setting you're in is another leg of that four-legged stool, and it's an important one. We'll talk a lot about that later on.

You also wouldn't want anyone to laugh at your questions, would you? Hey, what's worse than *that*? You finally get up the courage to ask a question and the guy in the front of the room looks at you like you like you're an idiot. He rolls his eyes and shakes his head and looks to the others for confirmation that you really *are* an idiot. And the others are more than willing to oblige him, *aren't* they?

Boy, that's probably the last time *you'll* open your mouth!

Am I right?

And if you were the student, you *certainly* wouldn't want the person teaching you to talk over your head, would you? No, you'd want that teacher to have a sense of your background and your education up to that point in your life. You wouldn't want that teacher to try to impress you by making you feel that he was so much smarter than you, would you?

But believe it or not, there are a lot of so-called teachers who do this every day of the week. Somebody should round up these people and make them all talk to each other for a couple of decades. I actually had one of these knuckleheads tell me that he felt it was his *duty* to humble the technicians by making them feel stupid. "When I'm done with them, Dan," he said, "I really don't care if they've learned anything. I just want them to know that they just listened to one smart man with a world of experience. I want them to leave my classroom in such a state of confusion that they'll have to depend on *me* for answers in the future. That's job *security*, Dan."

Put all of these bums in one big room, I say. Let 'em confuse *each other* for the rest of their lives.

I'll bet that if *you* were the student you'd probably want your teacher to be gentle with you. Wouldn't you?

So that's how you're going to succeed as a teacher of technicians – by doing and *being* all these things. All you have to do is treat others as you would have them treat *you*.

And let's face it, in this world, we are *all* teachers in one way or another. So let's spend the rest of our time together talking about how we can get *better* at it.

What makes technicians special?

First, they're used to moving around. Back in the days when they were being bored to tears by crummy school teachers they spent a lot of time staring out the window, longing to get *moving*. They wanted to get in a car or a truck and drive! They wanted to get out *there* where things were real and interesting and . . . fun!

As a teacher, it's your responsibility to keep things real, and interesting and fun.

If you don't, they'll be staring out that window all over again.

Technicians are very visual people. Technicians tend to think in pictures rather than in numbers and formulas. This is an important trait that most technicians have but other people often don't. A psychologist would call this talent "spatial reasoning." Technicians know where things are supposed to go before those things are actually in place. They see the job finished before they start. You can always spot a technician at a supermarket checkout. He'll be in a hurry to get going so he'll pack his own bags. Watch the way he puts the groceries into the bags. Everything fits perfectly. The eggs are on the top; the canned peaches are on the bottom. The bags are squared off and they're not too heavy. A technician can do that because he sees the future. What a remarkable talent that is!

As a teacher, it's your responsibility to make things very visual for the technicians in your charge. You do this by describing things in detail, by adding colors and shapes and detailed descriptions to everything you do. We'll talk more about this later. For now, just know that there's a difference between "a hammer," and "a five-pound sledge with a rusty head and an old wood handle that looks like it might snap the next time some poor guy gives it a good swing."

Do you *see* what I mean? That second "hammer" is a bit easier to visualize, isn't it? That's what I mean by "adding color." You can do that.

What else? Well, I've found that many technicians are loners. They don't play well with others. That's one of the things that led them into the field. They *like* to have a task to do. They prefer to do that task *alone*. And they usually like to do it as far away as possible from anything that looks like a boss.

Which means you'll also have to work on their people skills. Technicians can often be shy and sometimes a bit eccentric when it comes to dealing with customers. I knew this technician who had a thing about wiping his feet before entering a customer's home. One of his old bosses had pounded this into his head. "Don't track mud," he repeated over and over again.

Now, don't get me wrong; I'm all for wiping feet. That's common sense, and common courtesy, and none of us should be tracking mud into *anyone's* house. But as with so many things in life, you *can* carry the process to an extreme. This particular technician raised it to a fetish. He'd knock on the door and when the homeowner answered he would avert his eyes, staring at his own shoes, of course. He would state his purpose, and when invited to enter, he would begin to scuff the bottoms of his shoes on the doormat. He wouldn't just take two or three hits on that mat. No, he'd scuff away at that doormat like a dog that had just taken a monster load and needed to cover it for all time. He'd stand and scuff and never raise his eyes to look at the customer. If you were standing next to him, you tended to do the same thing. You just couldn't help it because his actions were contagious and pretty close to psychotic.

Before long, the customer went into an involuntary scuff from his side of the doorway. It was *very* unsettling.

This, then, also has to become a part of your teaching. You have to work on the people skills. But you have to weave this into the technical stuff. You can't just come out and say, "Hey, you don't know how to have a conversation because you're a loner!" Say that, and you'll make yourself a brand-new enemy – maybe even a *roomful* of brand-new enemies! No, you have to get this message across in a more gentle way. It's not difficult to do. You can start by telling some wild and crazy stories (maybe about a guy who scuffs his shoes?). I'll show you how to do this even better later on. Be patient.

Okay, what's next? Well, you're not going to like this very much but most technicians probably think they know a heck of a lot more than you do. They think this because they're "out there" and you're not. You may have been "out there" once upon a time, but you're not *now*, and that makes you less experienced with what's going on right now. At least to them.

They'll never tell you that, but it's true, and you know what? They may be right! And if they are, you'll have to recognize this and do something about it. Find a way to get more real-world experience if you need it. Travel with the technicians and find out what's happening nowadays. Work this into the knowledge that you already have and you'll be a more powerful teacher. You can't get through to technicians if they don't respect you. Give them reasons to respect your knowledge.

And you can't do this by hanging plaques around the room. With technicians, you have to be able to gain respect by talking the talk and walking the walk, and that means you have to stay current. Do this for *yourself*, as well as for them.

Okay, let's sum this up. Technicians are special. And because they *are*, there's a very good chance they'll turn you off and fall asleep if you don't do your job well.

So here's what you're going to do:

- You're going to think like they do.
- You're going to enter *their* world.
- You're going to see things as they see them.
- You're going to learn how to abandon mumbo-jumbo in favor of terms used by regular human beings.
- You're going to learn how to take the new concepts and connect them to things the technicians already know.
- You're going to bring to your teaching this elusive thing we call *fun*.
- And finally, you're going to accept that you're probably *not* going to be masterful at this right from the start. You didn't learn the technical aspects of your business overnight, did you?

So be gentle with yourself.

And patient.

CHAPTER ONE
We all have to start someplace, eh?

Be prepared!

I spent 19 years working for a manufacturers' representative on Long Island, New York. We sold heating equipment to wholesalers. Contractors bought that equipment from the wholesalers and installed it in both old and new buildings. There was a *lot* to that business, and there was no formal place where technicians could go to learn it all. Most of what they knew, they learned on the job from older technicians.

They had trade associations, of course. Some of these were better than others. Some associations were just places where you'd go to have a beer with the guys once a month. But other associations were much more serious about education. These groups would comb the industry, looking for speakers who would be willing to show up at a monthly meeting and talk for an hour or so about what they knew best. And since budgets were limited, most of these trade associations asked manufacturers and manufacturers' reps to do the speaking because these guys would willingly show up for free in hopes that they could get in some plugs for their products.

And so it was that I found myself in the basement of a Knights of Columbus hall on Long Island one winter's evening a long time ago. I was there with two salesmen from the company. They were about 20 years older than I was. They were *men*; I was a kid. I was just supposed to be there to learn a thing or two from these wizened old-timers. They were going to show me the ropes. They were going to demonstrate how much they knew, and how they could dazzle the technicians that had come to hear them speak that night.

Just before it was time for the old-timers to go on and enlighten us all, the younger of the two salesmen turned to the other guy and said, "Hey, I've got an idea! Let's let *Dan* do the talk tonight. It will be *good* for him. He's been with the company for, what, a year now? He should know his stuff well enough to get up there and talk for an hour to these technicians, don't you think? What do you say, Dan? Are you PREPARED?"

I looked at the old-timers, and then I looked at the fifty or so technicians that had come to get educated, and then I got sick to my stomach. I wasn't prepared to talk for two minutes, let alone an *hour*. I started to stammer and make excuses and *beg* them to do the talk. I simply wasn't prepared. They finally let me off the hook.

They had a good laugh at my expense that night, and they made me feel younger than I was. They also made me feel stupider than I probably was. Fear of public speaking can make you feel that way in a hurry. It was a pretty good lesson, though, because it was the first time I felt that sick feeling in the pit of my stomach that comes from not being prepared. It was *not* a good feeling to have, and I knew then that I didn't want to have that feeling again.

I've learned that the only way *not* to feel that way is to be prepared.

And be relevant

Some time passed after that embarrassing night and I learned a bit more. The manufacturers' rep I worked for had a service department and I hung around with the serviceman whenever I had free time. I'd ask him about the products we sold and what could go wrong with them. I figured he'd most likely know since he was fixing those products for a living. No one ever called this guy to tell him something was working just fine. He shared what he knew with me, but the peculiar thing about the knowledge he had was that it revolved around fixing things that had broken within the first year of installation. You see, we only did in-warranty service, and the warranty ran for just one year. After that, the customers were on their own.

So I was learning from a technician who specialized in fixing brand-new stuff that broke down right out of the box. This stuff was still relatively unmolested and basically squeaky clean. The bolts had not yet had a chance to bond chemically with the nuts. Things still came apart fairly easily. I listened to him, I traveled with him, and I learned from him.

And then we got to a point where my old boss decided that I was now bright enough to go out into the world and teach technicians what I had learned. "You've seen what goes wrong with our products, Dan," he said. "Sometimes the technicians don't install our products the right way. Get out there and show them a thing or two about how to do it properly."

I believe I was about 11 years old at the time.

Or at least that's how old I felt. I also believed I knew *everything* there was to know about these products. I had worked with them for a couple of years, after all! And I had traveled for a few days with the in-warranty serviceman who fixed brand-new stuff that had failed right out of the box hadn't I? What else was there to know?

I still remembered my experience with the wizened old-timers at the Knights of Columbus hall, however, so I made *sure* I had a canned speech all prepared, with notes and samples of brand-new stuff that had broken right out of the box, and everything else I could possible need. I even had chalk just in case I happened to run across a blackboard.

I was *ready*!

One of our salesmen knew a service manager from an oil company on Long Island. Our guy approached their guy and convinced him that it would be worthwhile for both him and his company to keep his technicians after work for a couple of hours. Sure, they'd have to pay the technicians overtime, but in return, the technicians would get to hear the pearls of wisdom from "one of the brightest young minds in the heating industry" – that being me.

There was also beer and pizza involved as I recall, which may or may not have had something to do with the technicians' willingness to stay after hours and listen to what some dopey kid had to say.

The service manager, being a good friend of our salesman and *also* a fan of pizza and beer, agreed to the suggestion and the meeting was set for a Tuesday night.

I showed up in a brand-new, three-piece suit with all these brand-new parts that had failed right out of the box within a year of installation. I also had all my brand-new notes, of course. They put me in a conference room with about 20 technicians. Some of those technicians could have been my father. Hell, some could have been my *grandfather*! Some looked like they had just played major roles in a Hell's Angels movie. Others looked like they could open the beer cans with their teeth (which, I soon learned, they *could*).

Anyway, they ate all the pizza and drank all the beer and then it was my turn to go on. I stood up before these dirty, hard-working technicians who had gotten up earlier than I had that morning and who had worked a lot harder than I had all day long. I stood there looking down on this group of men who looked like they had seen all the mechanical evil that there is to see in this whole world. And then I opened my mouth.

I don't remember exactly what it was that I said, but I *do* remember that after less than ten minutes, one of the technicians threw an empty beer can at me. Others followed with pizza crust and balled-up versions of my handouts. They started to belch and fart and talk to each other. They got up and stretched and threw some more stuff at me. I did my best to hang on, but then one guy (who turned out to be the Top Dog in that shop) stood and said, "*Hey*, you don't know your ass from third base, kid. Why don't you just shut up and let us get home at a decent hour tonight. We're all tired."

So I shut up, and they went home. This was the beginning of my *permanent* loss of ego. It never came back because I have steadfastly refused to forget that night. I use it as a constant reminder of where I came from. Today I can sit and write a book about this stuff, but I will *never* forget how terribly bad I once was at teaching.

Do you know what I did wrong that night? I didn't understand my audience. What I was bringing to them was something that wasn't relevant to what they were doing from day to day. I started out by telling them that most of what went wrong with our products was a result of how *they* installed the stuff.

Now, wasn't *that* just brilliant? There I was standing up in front of people who had seen much more that I had of both life and mechanical mayhem, and I started my talk by telling them that *they* were a bunch of screw-ups.

It's a wonder they didn't throw the *full* cans of beer at me.

A week or so later when the dust had settled, I swallowed what was left of my pride and I went back to see that service manager. I asked him if it would be possible for me to ride with his best technician for a few days. At first he laughed. I mean, I was standing there in a suit and my hands were as clean as a surgeon's. When he realized that I was dead serious, though, he agreed to let me travel with one of his guys. He told me to show up at their shop the next morning by 7 AM sharp – in work clothes. Don't wear sneakers.

I never asked my boss for permission to do this because I was afraid he wouldn't approve. I could have blown up some customer's house (and myself!) and there would probably have been a question of liability insurance somewhere in there. So I just committed a sin of omission and did it. I could get away with this because I was working on the road at the time and nobody knew where I was from minute to minute. Heck, *I* didn't know where I was from minute to minute!

The guy that the service manager sent me out with was one of the best technicians I had ever met. He made me do all the dirty work and I just kept my mouth shut and did as I was told. We traveled together for a few days and I learned a lot – both about the products I was selling, and about *his* world. I think about Bobby every time I got up in front of a group of technicians in the many years that followed. He was *always* on my mind when I was working. And even though I'm retired from teaching, I still want Bobby to be proud of me. He helped me to understand the importance of being relevant. You have to *live* it if you're going to speak about it. You don't have to live it *every* day, but you *do* have to live it.

After the Night of the Beer Cans, I repeated my "Travel with the Top Dog" experience over and over again with many different companies throughout Long Island, New York City, and New Jersey. I never once told my boss what I was doing for fear that he would have stopped me from getting my education. I traveled with, and learned from, some of the best technicians in my industry. I picked them from large and small companies, in both the city and the country, and I got *real* dirty.

And that's when I began to learn.

Ask <u>yourself</u> the questions first

The rep I worked for sold a lot of steam heating equipment, and I had studied this booklet that one of the manufacturers had published. It was all about steam heating and it was a pretty good booklet. I was young and trusting and somewhat stupid at the time. I honestly thought that this marvelous booklet contained everything anyone would ever want to know about steam heating. I read it again and again. Memorized it, in fact. Then I asked my boss if we could make a mailing to the local trade, inviting them to come to my inaugural steam heating seminar so that they could listen to me reveal the technical secrets they so longed to know.

I did this solely because I wanted to impress my boss. I figured if I was able to teach technicians a thing or two about steam heating, they would buy more stuff from the wholesalers we sold to. And when that happened, my boss would give me a raise.

That was my motivation, and to my delight, he agreed to the mailing and it was a big success. I managed to attract about 30 of the more prominent local technicians to my inaugural steam heating seminar. That was as many as would fit in our conference room. My boss was happy because not only were these people prominent, they also had agreed to pay $25 each for the privilege of hearing me preach for an entire day on a subject I was just beginning to love – that being steam heat. The collected monies covered the cost of the meeting. It was a *wash*! And what could be better than that? I was a teacher!

Or so I thought.

Anyway, the group arrived bright and early and I began my talk at exactly 9 AM. At precisely 10:15 AM (and I will *always* remember this because I glanced at my watch) I had shared *everything* that I knew about steam heating with the 30 prominent technicians in attendance. Unfortunately, I still had five hours and 45 minutes remaining in the seminar.

"Are there any questions?" I asked, hoping the group would have some answerable questions that I would be able to stretch until 4 PM, which at the time seemed as far away as next Friday.

Ray Combs, a local heating legend, whom I believe gnawed on a box wrench in his bassinet, raised his hand. "Dan," he said, "can you explain the difference between a condensate pump and a boiler-feed pump?"

Ray, of course, knew the answer to his own question, but he had a lesson of his own to teach that morning. I looked at him, and I felt as though Death had just kissed me on the lips.

"A condensate pump and a boiler-feed pump?" I said, never having heard of either device before that moment.

"That's right." Ray said, sighting over his reading glasses like a rifleman. "A condensate pump and a boiler-feed pump."

"Well, the difference is, umm . . . Yes, um, the difference is . . . Well, a condensate pump, um, pumps condensate? And a boiler-feed pump, I think it feeds a boiler?"

Ray sat there staring and letting me swing in the breeze for what felt like three hours.

"You don't *know* the difference, do you?" he finally said. "DO YOU?!"

I just shook my empty head because my brain could no longer make my mouth form words. I hadn't asked *myself* the questions these technicians might ask me. That's an important part of preparation, you know. You have to think like the technicians think, *and you have to anticipate every possible question they can ask you.*

I didn't know that at the time.

But here comes the *real* scary part. Ray stood up, casually strolled to the front of the room, and held out his hand for the chalk.

Which I gave him.

He then looked at me in a very sad way and he quietly said, "Take a seat in the back, kid. These people paid to be here. *I'll* tell them the difference between a condensate pump and a boiler-feed pump. Go ahead. Run along."

I tucked my tail between my legs and took Ray's seat in the back of the room. He then proceeded to teach the class for the rest of the day. Did a great job, too! My boss came in to watch for a while, and as the hours wore on, I got smaller and smaller. At one point, I think I disappeared entirely. I was irrelevant. But before I disappeared, I promised myself that this would *never* happen to me again. Any vestige of the ego that might have been left over from the Night of the Beer Cans and the Knights of Columbus Fright Festival was gone forever.

But that was the greatest lesson anyone has ever taught me about teaching. I will be forever grateful to Ray Combs for teaching it to me at such an early age, and in all the years that followed, before I began speaking, I looked for him in the audience. That man scared the crap out of me until the day he died, but he taught me that a teacher should *never* open his mouth in front of a group unless he or she knows the topic inside and out. And you *must* anticipate their questions because they *surely* will come. This is one of the most important parts of your preparation stage, as you shall see.

Some good places to begin

I swear by the Dale Carnegie Course. I took it when I was 21 years old and I will always remember that first night. I didn't know anyone in the room and I was painfully shy (which is why I was there). The teacher asked each of us to stand, say our name, and tell what we did for a living.

I couldn't do it.

I just sat there and squirmed.

A few weeks later, though, I couldn't sit down! Dale Carnegie is a life-changing experience and it's a *great* place to begin if you're serious about becoming a better teacher. They give you confidence and get you over the preliminary fear of speaking in public. They don't help you learn your subject, but they *do* make you want to get up and talk. Check them out at http://www.dalecarnegie.com

If you don't have the time or the money for Dale Carnegie, look into Toastmasters International (http://www.toastmasters.org). I belonged to this group for a couple of years and I had a ball. The dues were minimal and we met once a week at a local library. What you'll find at Toastmasters will be a bunch of nice people from all walks of life who want to get better at speaking in public. They're incredibly supportive of each other and you will get to give a short speech every week. You're going to *love* the applause!

When I was in my late twenties, and after I had been teaching technicians for a couple of years, my old boss sent me into New York City for a course titled, "The Professional Trainer." It was being given at the headquarters of the American Management Association in Manhattan, and I recall it was ridiculously expensive (as are *all* AMA courses).

There were about 20 of us in that class and the course material focused on how adults learn. This was fascinating stuff. I had never before considered that grown-ups learn in a way that's very different from the way kids learn. You can tell a kid something, and if it seems somewhat plausible, the kid will buy into it. Repeat it enough times and the kid will take it as gospel.

Adults are different. You have to *prove* it to adults. This is because they have much more experience in life and they've learned to be skeptical. Most adults have built-in, fine-tuned BS Detectors. You have to win their trust, and you have to *prove* that what you're saying is true.

And that makes all the difference in the world.

I recall the teacher gave us this great example of the different ways adults learn. She told us that some people could learn how to play golf by picking up a set of clubs and going right out on the course. These people have natural athletic ability. They just have a feel for the game and they're able to teach themselves.

Other people, however, have to hire a pro to show them what to do. There's no way they can just pick up the clubs and go. They need lessons from someone who is better than they are at this frustrating sport.

And then there are those annoying individuals who can actually learn how to play golf by watching a video or reading a book. They project themselves vicariously into the sport and get into the Zen of the thing. I always think of Chevy Chase in *Caddyshack* when I think of these folks.

The point being, we all learn in different ways. That's what makes teaching adults such a challenge. You have to approach your subject from a lot of different angles, bringing in the varied elements that can help adults learn. A good teacher will always come at a subject from several directions, showing pictures, telling stories, using props – bringing in sounds and sights, colors, and textures, and flavors.

That was a valuable lesson for me and I'm glad that I learned it early in my career. When I taught, I showed pictures on the screen as I painting more pictures with my words. My PowerPoint slides contained few if any words. I didn't want my students reading when I was talking to them. I used photographs or simple diagrams and we looked at these together.

I mixed in stories for those people who might be able to learn golf by reading a book or watching a video. I passed around products or props for those who need to have the thing in their hand to make the connection to their brain. I mixed as many ways as I could think of to get through to the maximum amount of adult technicians in that room.

And you know what's funny? The group didn't realize that I was doing this to them. This is part of the teacher's art. When done properly, it's seamless. People *learn*. You get through to them. And that's what counts. You make a difference in their lives. And they had *fun*.

The other thing they did for us at that American Management Association course was to videotape our speeches during that week. We had to watch our previous day's performance the first thing each morning, and we had to critique each other as well. This was a *brutal*, but absolutely valuable, experience. I learned what I was doing right and I learned what I was doing wrong. I also learned an awful lot about body language, which I'll share with you in a little while.

And in case you're wondering, people *do* look a lot heavier on TV. Oh, it's brutal!

Anticipate disaster!

So, are you ready to get up there and teach?

Well, don't be in such a rush. I have to toughen up your skin a bit before you head out there. It can get pretty scary in the real world, and things often don't go as planned. I've had just about every horrible thing that you can imagine happen to me while in the process of striving to save the world from mechanical mayhem. I've had to learn how to adapt, create and overcome under the worst circumstances. I had to deal with Mother Nature, the hotels of North America, and the more than 200,000 people that I taught before retiring in 2016.

Here, I'll tell you about a few things that have happened to me. This should make you feel a *lot* better.

When it *absolutely, positively* has to be there overnight! I flew to Saginaw, Michigan to speak to 75 eager technicians. I assumed the stuff I had sent ahead by Federal Express had flown there the day before I did.

It hadn't.

This is why I have learned that you *never, ever* send something that you can't afford to be without to a meeting. Anticipate *disaster*. If the meeting can't go on without something, *carry it with you*, and *never* let it out of your sight. If *you* make it to the meeting, the stuff also makes it. If you *don't* make it, well, then it really doesn't matter, does it?

FedEx found the package nine months later . . . and then sent it to Saginaw.

And by the way, while returning from this jaunt to beautiful Saginaw, Michigan, I managed to tear the entire back out of my chinos while sliding into the middle seat of a 737 jet airplane. I had to slide into my seat because the big guy in the aisle seat refused to stand up and let me get by. It was an old plane and it had this razor-sharp hunk of metal sticking out of the armrest. It took out the back of those chinos as neat as can be. I had a full-blown trapdoor that displayed my butt to that entire, overbooked aircraft. I was, needless to say, assigned to the front of the plane. You know that song, "Moon Over Miami?" Well, this was "Moon Over *Michigan*."

And it wasn't a direct flight, of course. Did I mention that? Oh noooo, I had a two-hour layover at Chicago's O'Hare airport, and the connecting flight was delayed (that goes without saying, right?). I couldn't even cover my big butt because I had left my stinking jacket back at the hotel in Saginaw.

So I slid along the wall at O'Hare International Airport for several hours while tolerating the snickering of the masses of people that passed through.

You *can't* plan for stuff like this. All you can do is adapt, create, and hopefully, overcome.

Water water everywhere. You're about to start your talk, but you want to make that one last trip to the bathroom because you're a bit nervous and you've had about seven cups of coffee. You have about five minutes to go before Show Time. You do your business and you scurry over to the sink to wash your hands. What you don't know is that some bozo has removed the aerator from the sink's spout. And did I mention that the town you're speaking in has about 750 pounds per square inch of city water pressure?

Before you can shout "Man overboard!" you have half of the state's water supply dripping from the groin area of your tan slacks.

Time to go on!

There is a similar situation known as the Condensation Lap Drip. Let's say they've asked you to give an after-dinner talk at that big fancy association banquet. It's a hot night and the air-conditioning isn't what it ought to be. You take one last sip of that ice water before getting up to share your wisdom with the congregation. You tip the glass toward your lower lip and about a gallon of condensation runs from the outside of your glass and lands with a splash (you guessed it!) on the groin area of your tan slacks. There's no lectern to hide behind, of course. "Look! There's a man who's so nervous he just peed in his pants. Imagine that."

Mad dogs and air conditioners. If the room has an air conditioner, that air conditioner will most likely break down on the hottest day of the year. And that's the day you will be speaking to the technicians, of course. You'll probably be gathered together in the Louisiana bayou, the Sahara Desert, or hell.

This happened to me once in Connecticut. I had a roomful of technicians at some hotel and the AC was vomiting hot air from the ceiling. The hotel staff said they were working on it, but I think I had all the HVAC technicians in town in that room, so they weren't able to get any of them on the phone.

We opened the doors that led to the parking lot, hoping to stir up a breeze. As soon as I did this, a Doberman charged into the room and bit one of my guys on his thigh. No kidding. This is the sort of thing that can happen when the air-conditioning breaks. Who figures on this?

Anyway, the dog was growling and chewing, and the technician was yelping and trying to pry the beast off his leg. A bunch of us finally managed to beat the dog off the guy. The dog ran out the door and we were all standing there in shock. Before I could get the door closed, a 15-pound crow soared into the room and started auditioning for the remake of Alfred Hitchcock's *The Birds*.

I hope that never happens to you, but anticipate that it might. Because it *can*.

Power outages. I've had the electricity blow out *dozens* of times, of course. That's expected, and it will always happen at the worst possible time. I've even gone to hotels where there was no electricity at all in the room. I set up the projector and then looked around for a place to plug in.

"Where's the outlet?" I asked the night clerk, who was on the last half-hour of his shift.

"There ain't no outlet in that room," he said, never looking up from his newspaper.

"What am I supposed to do?" I asked, exasperated. "I have a bunch of technicians coming for a meeting and I have to have electricity. Where am I supposed to plug in?"

"Didn't you bring a long extension cord?" he asked. He looked at me as though I were the dumbest guy in the state. "The Rotary Club never asks for an outlet," he said. "And they meet here once a week."

Night clerks all have the same mother.

Under construction. If you're hiring a hall to give your speech, make sure the place isn't going to be under construction. This happens a lot more than you might think. I was talking to a group of technicians in Canada once and a couple of hotel employees were building a wall right next door. The hammering and sawing was pretty distracting. We complained to the hotel people and they stopped the employees from working until our meeting was over. They were pretty cooperative.

Another time, though, I wasn't so lucky. My company had booked a hotel in Rhode Island for a full-day seminar for over 100 technicians. What we didn't know (and we *should* have asked about this in advance) was that there was a multilevel parking garage directly under our meeting room. There was a demolition crew jackhammering the concrete all day long. It sounded like a war zone in that meeting room, and there was no way the hotel could get the contractor to stop because those contractors weren't hotel employees. We got *nowhere* with those people. The part that made me nuts was that the hotel staff *knew* weeks before our meeting that there was going to be construction right under our meeting room, but they never said a word to us.

No excuses, though. I should have asked. After that day, I always did.

Hurricanes. I once went on a seminar tour through New England. I was traveling exactly one day behind a vicious hurricane that had trashed a large part of Connecticut, Massachusetts, and Rhode Island. The hotel where I was scheduled to speak got their power back just minutes before I was to go on.

The weather can be pretty unpredictable.

Music, music, music! I once began a seminar in Pennsylvania only to learn that the hotel had booked a gospel choir into the next room. Ten minutes into my talk, the walls began to boom as eighty, robed, sweaty, overweight, clapping, howling women commenced to whooping and hollering about Jesus and the Promised Land.

I should have asked about this beforehand. I always asked about this afterwards.

In Connecticut it was a country/western band with their amplifiers cranked up to #11. Yeeee *Ha*! "Can you turn it *down* a bit?" I shouted at the guy in the ten-gallon hat who looked just like Hoss Cartwright from the old *Bonanza* TV show. "Hell *no!*" he screamed back at me. *"We're here to rock the house, pardner!"*

I should have asked about Hoss *beforehand*.

So should you.

Crossed wires. You've got a microphone. The guy doing the talk in the next conference room has a microphone. Sound normal so far, right? It's not. That other guy's microphone is wired to *your* speakers. And vice versa, of course. I'm giving a lecture on steam heating to a group of middle-aged women in the next room. The guy next door is telling your technicians how to seek happiness by overcoming low self-esteem. The hotel says the engineer is on vacation and there's *nothing* they can do about it.

This actually happened to me. And the best part was two timid ladies approached the sign-in table and softly ask if this was the esteem seminar. My assistant thought they were saying steam seminar and she let them in.

You can't make this stuff up.

This electrical flip-flop also happens with room lights, of course. You turn off the switch in your room to show some slides and nothing happens – but the lights go out in the other guy's room.

And vice versa, of course.

The shape of things to come. One time a seminar booking service sent me to a hotel in northern-New Jersey. They had booked this place from a thousand miles away without ever seeing it. The room they chose was shaped like the capital letter L. Half of the 120 technicians sat around the corner from where I was. At six-thirty that morning, the hotel folks smiled sadly at me and said, "Do the best you can, Mr. Holohan."

We had to rearrange all the furniture at the last minute and this is why you should *always* demand to see the room you're going to be working in the night before the meeting. Don't wait until the last minute. Your room just might be shaped like the letter W.

Feeling hot, hot, hot! When I started teaching, overhead projectors were the way to go. They were so much nicer than blackboards. But I quickly learned that projector bulbs will blow at the worst possible time. And since overhead projectors are now antiques, you may not know that the bulb inside that ancient machine burns at a temperature that approximates the inside of the sun. I once grabbed hold of one of these bulbs a second after it had blown. I was young and quite stupid at the time. In a nanosecond, that little hunk of hell raised two, water balloon-sized blisters on my thumb and index finger. I screamed and launched into the Dance of Pain, much to the delight of the technicians who were sitting there watching.

I flung the bulb into a nearby plastic garbage pail. It immediately burned through the plastic and set fire to the rug. I danced the Dance of Pain on the flaming rug and waved my two water balloons in the air – all to the glee of those guys.

Along the same lines, I was speaking on the subject of radiant heating at the New Hampshire Plumbing-Heating-Cooling Contractors' convention. I heated up a brick on a hotplate until it practically glowed. This is what's known as "a prop." I removed the brick/prop, using a potholder to protect my hands from water balloon-sized blisters, and then I stupidly put it down on glass plate. A few seconds later, the plate exploded, showering the first row of people with glass shrapnel. My brain went into overdrive. I grabbed the white-hot brick with my bare hand (YEOW!) and set it down on a hunk of Styrofoam insulation, which immediately burst into flames. The New Hampshire PHCC members actually *enjoyed* this. They thought it was part of the show.

And in a miserable way, I suppose it was.

No-shows. I got hired once to go to Connecticut to do a hot-water-heating seminar. A manufacturers' rep and a wholesaler jointly sponsored this one. They booked a meeting room in a hotel and figured that at least 100 people would attend. The rep assumed the wholesaler was going to do all the promotional work – the mailings, the phone calls, and all the other details that go into getting a big group of technicians together in one place at the same time. The wholesaler, unfortunately, assumed the opposite. He figured the rep was doing all the legwork.

Turns out, neither of them did anything.

I showed up that morning and these two Masters of Organization had exactly two technicians sitting in the meeting room.

"What do you want to do?" I asked. The guy from the rep agency and the wholesaler were both middle-management types, and neither wanted to tell their bosses that they had put together everything *except* an audience. So they both said, "Do the seminar, Dan. We'll pay you nevertheless. Let's just keep this as our little secret."

So I lectured for eight hours to two guys who *insisted* on sitting in the back row. They figured that if they sat up front I might call on them or something. They were trying to hide from the teacher. That's why they sat in the back. There was nothing between them and me except 98 empty chairs, but these two knuckleheads wouldn't budge. They were so far away I thought they were sitting in Rhode Island. At lunch, we had more waitresses than diners because the rep and the wholesaler had also ordered (and paid for) enough food to feed Nebraska.

On that day it became my official policy to *never* speak to groups of less than two. I maintained that policy until the day I retired.

You can't have a meeting without an audience. Make a note of that somewhere.

No room at the Inn. I drove into the parking lot of the Holiday Inn in Glenwood Springs, Colorado late one summer night and was greeted by a marquee that read, "Holiday Inn Welcomes Dan Holohan!" I tapped my friend John Geiger on the arm to make sure he knew that he was traveling with a big shot. John just shook his head and smiled.

We went to the front desk to check in. John got his room right away. When it was my turn to check-in, the night clerk told me that he had no reservation for a Dan Holohan. "Just give me *any* room," I said. He smiled an evil grin and told me there *were* no rooms – either here or at any other hotel within a hundred miles of beautiful Glenwood Springs, Colorado. "This is our *busy* season . . . sir." Then he burped. He actually burped! "Your people should have made a *reservation* for you . . . sir."

I dragged the guy outside and pointed at the bright marquee. "That's *me*!" I said. "*I'm* Dan Holohan! I'm up on your marquee! I came all the way from New York to Colorado to give a *speech*. I want a room!"

"You could be Elvis brought back to life, sir," he said, and belched. "I *still* wouldn't have a room for you tonight."

I slept on a cot with the mops and the brooms that night.

Lesson learned? *Always* get a confirmation number – *especially* at the Holiday Inn.

Let's get ready to rumble! Three times I had fights break out at my seminars, and three times I have had to wade into the middle of them to break things up. And I'd like you to appreciate that these were not mere verbal altercations. No, we're talking full-blown hockey fights here. And it doesn't take much to get one going. A technician's big butt knocks a pitcher of ice water off the table and into another technician's lap and it's off to Round One. Bam! Another time a technician in the sixth row flicks the ear of a technician in the fifth row while mentioning that the question the technician in the fifth row just asked was a stupid one. The technician in the sixth row knows the technician in the fifth row casually, and he thinks the ear flicking is all in good sport. He is wrong, and we're off to Round Two. Whack!

My favorite fight, however, was the third one. This one took place in New York City (the other two fights took place in suburbs of New York, in case you're wondering). I was talking to a mixed group of technicians and engineers about steam heating. There was this engineer in the first row that wouldn't let me get through a complete paragraph. He picked every nit he could. "*Excuse* me," he'd say. "I *beg* to differ. It's not *exactly* like that." And then he would turn around and speak directly to the audience. No one knew what the heck this guy was saying but he sure seemed to like to hear himself talk.

After an hour or so of this I politely asked him to hold his comments for the break when he could have 100 percent of my time. "*Excuse* me," he said. "I *paid* to be here and *I'll* ask questions whenever *I* please."

I didn't know what to say, but as it turned out, I didn't have to say much at all. A big, burly technician sitting next to the guy turned to him and said, "Excuse *me*! I paid to be here *too*, and I'd like to hear what Dan has to say." The engineer turned around and looked the contractor up and down as though he was something scraped from a shoe. "You mind your own *business*," the engineer said. "Excuuuuuse *me*," the technician answered, and then planted a fist the size of a ham hock on the engineer's nose. The results, as you can imagine, were quite sloppy.

You adapt. You create. You overcome.

What's in a name? I scheduled a seminar at a hotel near Newark International Airport, which is in the Garden State of New Jersey. Everything was going splendidly until the hotel folks decided to change the name of their hotel. They made this decision on the day before my seminar was to take place. They didn't tell *anyone* they were going to do this. Seventy-six people struggled to find a hotel that didn't exist that morning – me being one of them.

Call ahead.

It's up there *someplace*! If you're using a screen at your meeting you'll want to make sure that all the technicians will be able to see the image you project. The bigger the audience, the bigger the screen needs to be. Common sense, right? And with a big screen you also need a tall ceiling. Also common sense.

Right?

Anyway, a meeting planner booked a hotel for me in central Massachusetts once. The hotel folks assured the meeting planner that the ceiling height was 12 feet in the room we were renting. That was very important to me because of the size of the group. I got there and looked up. The ceiling was exactly 10 inches above my head. When I inquired as to the location of the other five feet of air space, the catering manager lifted a ceiling tile and pointed upward. "There it is," he said.

What can you do?

Fifteen minutes after I started talking that morning the room went on fire and we had to evacuate. We were on the top floor. (I've had meeting rooms go on fire three times in my career. Fires can seriously throw off your timing.)

Going up? Later on, I'm going to show you a specification we use when we book a hotel for a meeting. You'll notice that we ask for a meeting room on the ground floor. Can you guess why? It's not just because of the fires. It's because the elevator will be broken on the morning of your meeting. The meeting room will be 100 feet above your head, and you'll be carrying a bunch of heavy stuff up a lot of stairs.

And then the arriving technicians will tell you about their bad knees.

Road work. The day I did a seminar for 75 technicians in Wilkes-Barre, PA, the City of Wilkes-Barre decided to pave all of the streets surrounding the conference center. My people, along with 1,000 people from Pennsylvania Power and Light, who were coming for a luncheon, had a tough time getting to the building that day. This also throws off your timing.

It's difficult to anticipate stuff like this. Just *know* that it happens.

***Your* schedule vs. *their* schedule.** I parked my car in the municipal parking garage next to a hotel in Syracuse, New York. I checked in, took a good long look at the meeting room, had dinner, and went to bed. The next morning I got up early to unload my van and set up the seminar.

That's when I learned that the City of Syracuse locks that particular parking garage at night. They open it when they're damn good and ready to open it, and the next time I go to Syracuse, I will be *sure* to unload the contents of my van into my hotel room the night before.

And in the years that followed, I *always* asked the guys in *every* parking garage I entered what time they closed, and what time they open in the morning.

And those are just the highlights. The life of a traveling teacher is *anything* but dull. And even if you never leave your hometown, a lot can *still* go wrong. Anticipate disaster.

Prepare.

CHAPTER TWO
The greatest fear of all

Butterflies?

The average person would rather have root canal work done than get up in front of a group of people and give a speech. How about that?

Researchers learned long ago that public speaking is the greatest fear that people have. Many folks are more afraid of this than they are of death. I used to be one of those people. You know how I got over my fear? By *doing* it. There's really no substitute for doing it. Practice makes you better, and it takes away *most* of the fear. You'll probably never get rid of all of it, but practice is the best way to get over the fear of having all those eyes trained on you.

I've spoken to more than 200,000 technicians, but until the day I retired, I *still* got nervous when I stepped up to the plate. I've come to understand and actually *appreciate* that feeling in the pit of my stomach. It almost always goes away right after I begin. After a while, I looked forward to the queasiness. I thought of it as my edge. It made me sharper. It made me concentrate. It made me want to work hard and push past it. It made me want to take control. In fact, if I wasn't a bit nervous before a speech, I usually wound up being flat that day.

So don't fear the nervousness. Welcome it as your ally. It's perfectly normal to have butterflies in your stomach. The trick is to make them soar like the Blue Angels in perfect formation.

You're not really talking to a crowd

When you watch the news on TV don't you get the feeling that the person reading the news is talking just to *you*? You don't feel like a part of an enormous crowd, do you? No, it's personal.

Now consider what that newsreader is going through. She's sitting at a desk in a TV studio. She's reading the scrolling text off a teleprompter. There's someone in a control room who is matching the speed of the scrolling to the pace at which she's reading.

She's probably thinking about *one person* while she's reading. She may be thinking about a loved one. Or she may be thinking about some man or woman she saw on the street that morning when she came to work. She's probably *not* thinking that she's talking to *all* of America. And if he is, my guess is she's visualizing "America" as a single human being.

And that's why she makes the big bucks. She talks to just one person. She talks to you. And that's a good thing because when you think about it, only one person at a time is watching and listening to her.

Consider what you're doing right now. You're reading a book that I wrote a while ago. You probably feel like I'm right there speaking to you, don't you? *Sure* you do! I'm trying my best to make the words I'm putting in your head sound like a conversation between just the two of us.

I'm not writing to a big group. I'm writing to *you*. Just you. I have a picture of you in my mind's eye right now, and that picture has been there since the first page. Right now, I don't care about anyone else who might read this book in the future. I'm just here for *you*.

Can you feel it?

Good.

Now, when I would get up in front of a crowd, I would get nervous at first, as I told you before. But then I would remind myself that the crowd is made up of *individuals*. They're there together, sure, and they *do* look like a big hunk of humanity, but the truth is they're just individuals who happen to be sitting together in a big room.

And with that in mind, I would do exactly what I'm doing right now. *I would talk to just one person at a time.* There could be 500 people in that room, but I would talk to just one person at a time. And that's why I don't get nervous beyond those first few minutes.

I'm *not talking* to a crowd.

I'm talking to *you*.

Here's how to get into that one-on-one frame of mind

About 15 minutes before you start, go off somewhere and stretch. Reach down and touch your toes. Go through the same routine you'd do to prepare yourself for some aerobic exercise. This will help to relax you. If you don't know how to stretch properly, get a book about stretching. Don't work up a sweat; just take a few good stretches to loosen the long muscles in your arms and legs.

Now yawn. I'm serious about this. Yawning also helps you to relax. If you don't think you can yawn at will, you're mistaken. Here's how to do it (I learned this as a little kid and it works *every* time).

First, close your eyes. Then put your lips together and slowly let your jaw drop without letting your lips part. You'll feel the yawn coming almost immediately. Go with it. You'll look pretty silly while you're doing this, so try to do it in private.

Now, just before you go on, and after you've yawned a few times, take a couple of deep breaths. Breathe with your belly – in through your nose for a count of six, and then breathe out through your mouth for the same count of six. This will also help you to relax.

Now, shake your arms to loosen up a bit more and then smile as broadly as you can. That smile is going to set the tone for your whole talk. It's very hard to have negative feelings when you're smiling.

So smile!

Now, when you get up there in front of that group of technicians, think about that newsreader. Remember that even though there are a lot of people there, they are listening to you as individuals. You are *not* talking to a crowd. Imagine that you're sitting in a room with just *one* of those people. You're about to explain something to that one person. You're not nervous when you're speaking to just one person you really like are you? Of course you're not! So why be nervous now? Just make believe you're speaking to one person at a time. You know more about your subject than *any* one person in that room, don't you? Sure you do. That's why you're up there. *You're* the teacher.

So relax.

Now, as soon as you start your talk, I want you to find a few people in that room who are giving you the most positive energy. These will be the people who are nodding at just about everything you say. They're smiling at you. They're hanging on your every word. Talk to *these* people for the rest of the day.

If the crowd is large, pick out about four people. Try to get one person on either side of the room, another in the front of the room, and one in the back. Take turns speaking to each of them. Move your eyes around the room as you focus on these four people. Do this, and every single person in that room will think you're speaking to *them* as individuals. They're following your eyes. They're feeling like you care about *them* as individuals. Before long, you'll be getting positive energy from most of the people in that room. They'll have no idea that you're speaking to just four people.

I used this trick for years. I could speak to a crowd of 500 people. At the end of my talk some of those people would come up to the front of the room to shake my hand and tell me that they really learned a lot and had a great time. I'd look at that person and suddenly realize that I'm seeing him or her for the first time that day. They were there in the room all day, but I was talking to *my four people*. My eyes saw all the people, sure, but my mind was focused on just the four. To me, it was like being out to dinner with four close friends.

Here's another analogy that will help you understand this technique. Imagine you're at a ballgame in a crowded stadium, or at a sold-out rock concert. You have seats in the nosebleed section, so you've brought along a pair of binoculars. Before the game or the concert begins, you're using the binoculars to scan the crowd. You're focusing in on tiny groups of individuals. You're looking for a few friends that you know have tickets in better seats. Suddenly, you find them! As you watch them through the binoculars, you get sort of involved in what they're doing, don't you? They're getting themselves settled into their seats. They're chatting with each other. They're smiling and looking around. They look up in your direction occasionally.

And all the while you're doing this, you are sitting in a crowd of tens of thousands of people. But while you're looking through the binoculars, you lose the sense of that big crowd, don't you?

Okay, now stand up, keep the binoculars up to your eyes, *and talk to just that small group*. Talk to your friends, one on one.

That's what you're doing when you pick the four positive people out of that big audience. Suddenly, you're not speaking to a crowd anymore. You're focusing on a couple of friendly individuals. Try it because it *works*. It is the one of the best ways I know of to get over the fear of speaking in front of a big crowd.

Just relax and don't worry. You're among friends.

Feedback

The reason why you pick out the positive people when you first start talking is because you don't want anyone or anything to distract you at the beginning. Rest assured there will be negative people in that crowd. There *always* are. Don't dwell on them. Focus, at first, on the ones that are supportive. The negative people will stop being negative after a while if you're well prepared and doing a good job.

And encourage feedback while you're giving your talk. Come right out and ask for it. "How are you doing? Are you with me? Are you following what I'm saying? Did you understand that last point?" Ask them directly; they'll answer you and that will make you even better.

I once got hired to do a steam-heating seminar in a part of the country where there isn't that much steam heating. I had about 100 technicians in the audience and they were very, very serious. I stood up front talking like a Long Island boy and joked with them for a while. In between the jokes and stories there was a *lot* of technical stuff about steam heating flowing out toward them. I went on for a while longer but then I started to get concerned because this group was unusually quiet – like *mortuary* quiet. I began to wonder if they understood what the heck I was talking about.

So I asked them.

"Do you understand what I'm talking about?" I said. There was silence. "Am I getting through to you?" Silence. "Am I going too fast?" Nothing. "Too slow?" Absolute silence. They started to look at each other. "Are you happy with your lives?"

Nothing.

"Who was your favorite Spice Girl?"

That got me a couple of subdued laughs. Good.

I walked away from the front of the room and into the middle of the group. This is a neat technique because it makes you one of them. Suddenly, "the teacher" was gone and I was just Dan – just another guy in the crowd. I stood there for a moment and didn't say anything. They all looked at me. The ones in the front of the room turned so they could see what I was doing. That also changed the dynamics of what was happening in the room. When the technicians in the front of the room turned around to see me, they could also see the faces of the people seated behind them, and vice versa. The mood shifted subtly. It was almost like taking a break.

"Okay," I said. "I realize you're all having a tough time answering those questions I was asking. Maybe you're not sure if you're happy with your lives. Maybe you don't know if I'm talking too fast or too slow. Heck, *I'm* not even sure who my favorite Spice Girl is! I sort of like Posh, but Baby is pretty cute. Just can't decide. So I'll tell you what. I'm going to ask you a question that you can't *possibly* get wrong. And when you get this one right, you're going to feel very, very good about yourself. Are you ready?"

They all started to smile.

I took a ballpoint pen from my back pocket and held it high over my head. "Okay, here comes the big question. It's a fill-in-the-blank question. Now, look at the object in my right hand and fill in the blank." I waved the pen over my head, and very slowly said, "This . . . is . . . a . . .?". When I got to the last word, I didn't say it, but instead, pursed my lips and shook my head, as though the word "PEN!" was about to explode from my mouth.

They looked at me.

Finally, one guy said, "Pen."

"*Thank you!*" I shouted and ran toward him. I stood there and shook his hand like it was a pump handle. "Congratulations!" I shouted. "You took a *chance*, and you got it *right*! That's the sort of spirit that *built* this great nation. How do you feel?"

"Pretty good!" he said with a smile.

"I'll *bet* you do!" I said. "See what happens when you take a *chance*? It's like the lottery, isn't it? You gotta be in it to win it!" I pointed to guy sitting next to my guy and said, "*You* could be feeling as good as your buddy here, but *you* didn't want to take a chance, did you?" The second guy starts to smile and laugh. "You *knew* it was a pen, didn't you?" He nods. "But you thought that maybe Holohan was slipping a mechanical pencil in there, *right*? You figured I was just playing a trick on you, didn't you? Look at this face? Have you ever *seen* such a sincere face? I'd *never* substitute a mechanical pencil for a pen! It goes against *everything* I believe in. No, you didn't want to take a chance, and *that's* why you don't feel as good as your buddy does right now! Next time, *GO FOR IT!*"

I *ran* back up the front of the room and shouted, "Okay, we're going to try it again and this time, I encourage you *all* to live dangerously. Take a chance! You gotta be in it to win it!" I grabbed the glass of water that was on the lectern and held it high over my head. "This . . . is . . . a . . . glass . . . of . . . ?"

In unison, they shouted, "WATER!"

"Nope," I said, taking a gulp. "It's *vodka*. One-hundred-fifty proof." I took another big gulp.

The whole place cracked up. "You people are going to drive me to *drink* if you don't start talking to me," I said, taking another gulp. "We're all just a bunch of guys in a room. Let's talk to each other and have some fun today."

"Now about this steam heating business," I continued. "Do you understand the things I've told you so far?"

We were fine for the rest of the day. We didn't just break the ice. We dropped an anvil through it.

This is the sort of thing you can do with a group of technicians when you're willing to have fun, and when you're not afraid of feedback.

During my seminars, I would regularly stop and ask, "Are you having a good time?" When they nod, I'll say, "That's good! You know, I don't care if you learn anything today; I just want you to have a good time. That's why we're here. To have *fun*!" And then I would teach them like crazy. I'd slip all this technical stuff in between my stories and turn it into a big delicious knowledge sandwich.

I'd also stop from time to time when I sensed that things were getting a bit too heavy on the technical side and say, "Can I get you anything? Would you like a back rub? We have people who come in here to do that, you know. Just say the word. Or how about a big cold beer? A raise from your boss? Just say the word. I'm *here* for you, pal! Within reason, that is."

They'd start laughing. The whole mood changed. I'd smile my biggest smile and with a *most* sincere catch in my voice say, "You guys are *so* special to me. You had me at hello. You *complete* me!"

The whole place would crack up, and we'd move on from there with *everyone* smiling, and ready for some more technical stuff. This technique has you pushing at them and then backing off with some humor. You just ebb and flow all day long. Techie stuff. A story. More techie stuff. A clean joke. A short break. Back at it. It's like driving a car over a series of hills. You'll give it some gas, and then you'll let up a bit, then a bit more gas. After awhile, you start to sense exactly when to press down, and when to back off.

It becomes second nature and it feels very natural. You'll see.

Understanding how adults learn

Here's a statistic that might surprise you. The typical adult will forget 93% of what he has learned within 72 hours of learning it. If you went to my seminar on a Monday morning, by the following Thursday afternoon you would remember only 7% of what I spent a whole day telling you.

Hey, I've built an entire business around that statistic! That's why so many people kept coming back to my seminars. They forget what the heck I told them the first time around and they needed to hear it again. Some folks don't even remember that they were there!

Seriously though, this is why it's *so* important for you to encourage the technicians to take notes. Some will balk at that, but you *must* encourage them to write things down. There's a direct connection between the hand and the brain. Most technicians will tell you that the best way to learn how to fix something is to pick up the tools and do it themselves. What the hand touches, the brain remembers. It's one of the best ways to learn. Put a pen or a pencil in your hand (the tool) and watch how your retention rate soars.

Hit them with that statistic early on in the day: The typical adult will forget 93% of what he has learned within 72 hours of learning it. Reinforce this by dropping a fact on them somewhere early on that's a bit tough to remember. Make it a formula or something that has some numbers in it. Wait an hour and then ask them to repeat it back. Someone in your group will look down at his notes and repeat it. *Praise* that person. Walk over and pat him on the back. Make a big deal about how *this* guy didn't have to remember because *this* guy wrote it down. Explain that *this guy* has freed up his memory cells for more important matters. He has discovered the secret that separates an ordinary technician from an extraordinary technician. He doesn't have to remember everything *because he knows where to find it.*

Do this a couple of times early in the day and watch how they all start to take notes. It works. All you have to do is show the technicians what's in it for *them*. Explain to them that once they put something in their head they *own* it. No one can ever take it away. If they change jobs, that knowledge goes with them. It increases their value in the marketplace. It makes their lives easier. And if they write it down, the chances of that knowledge staying in their heads improves *significantly* because what the hand touches, the brain remembers.

Technicians *know* that this is true. They work with tools. Your job as a teacher of technicians is to help them make that connection to note taking.

The importance of analogies

Now, here's the key to *truly* understanding how adults learn:

You must attach what they *don't* know to what they *do* know.

It's that simple.

To do this properly, you have to make analogies. I've done this to you a number of times already in this book. Remember when I asked you to imagine that you were at a ballgame or a rock concert and I had you watching your friends through a pair of binoculars? Remember?

That's an analogy.

I also described the talent that most technicians have for spatial reasoning (a psychology term) by describing how well they can pack a bag of groceries at the supermarket. I *know* you've been to a grocery store, but I'm not sure whether you've ever studied psychology.

So I made my point with an analogy.

I'll be giving you analogies all throughout this book because in our relationship right now, I'm *your teacher*. Some day you'll probably teach me a thing or two, but right now, I'm doing my best to tie things you might not know to things that you *do* know. I'm doing this to make *you* a better teacher.

My specialty is hydronic heating (that's heating with hot water or steam). In a hot-water heating system there is a centrifugal pump that moves the water through pipes from the boiler to the radiators. We call this pump a "circulator."

Now, when I'm teaching hydronics to technicians I will always take the time to make the analogy between a circulator in a closed-loop, hydronic heating system and the motor on a Ferris wheel. The Ferris wheel motor doesn't have to actually "lift" the people up in the air; it just has to overcome the friction that's keeping the wheel from turning. The weight of the people coming down will balance the weight of the people going up.

The circulator in the heating system does the same thing. Water fills all the pipes in the system, so the weight of the water coming down will balance the weight of the water going up. And by getting the technicians thinking about a Ferris wheel (that which they *know*), I can help them understand how a circulator works (that which they may *not* know).

I've used the air pump at my local gas station to explain the principle of how high pressure goes to low pressure. Always.

I've equated radiant-floor heating to the way the curtain on the sunny side of an airplane gets hot, even though we're flying at 34,000 feet and the air outside is way below zero degrees.

So as a teacher of technicians, regardless of your topic, it is your responsibility to constantly observe life, looking for analogies to the things you're trying to teach. And you won't have to look that far because the world is *filled* with analogies.

Look around. Find them. *Use* them.

The unasked question

Most adults are reluctant to ask questions. You know why? It's because we reach a certain age when we're supposed to *know*. We have kids, right? The kids are constantly asking us questions. We're the grown-ups and that means we're supposed to have all the answers.

Even when we don't. When you're not sure, you probably *never* say you're not sure, right? You say "Go ask your mother."

We're supposed to know it all. We're grown-ups.

So then we get in a situation at work where someone asks us a technical question and we're not sure of the answer, we fake it. And then we don't even take the time to find the right answer because we don't know who to ask. Besides, to ask is to reveal that we don't know.

And that could be dangerous!

So we play this game with each other. *No one* has all the answers, but most adults simply don't know *how* to ask. They wind up faking it. And when a technician is faking it, it can get *really* dangerous.

I mentioned that my specialty is steam and hot water heating. In the world of steam heating we deal with this control called a pressuretrol (which is short for "pressure control"). It sits atop the steam boiler and tells the burner at what system pressure it should start and at what system pressure it should stop. The technician has to set the thing.

Now, if you read the instructions that come with a pressuretrol you'll learn that you can set the control to come on "at the desired pressure" and go off "at whatever pressure is required." Those are the actual words the manufacturers use in their instructions.

The trouble with the instructions, though, is that they don't tell you what those pressures should be. It's whatever you desire, and whatever is required.

When I was first learning about steam heating this confused me, so I called a boiler manufacturer and asked what the pressure should be. The guy on the other end of the phone said, "Set it for whatever pressure you need."

"But what if I don't *know* what pressure I need?" I asked.

"You have to know the pressure in order to set it," he said.

"Do *you* know what it should be?" I asked.

"Whatever it takes," he said.

You know why we were having this inane conversation? Because *neither* one of us knew the answer. We just jerked each other around for a while because we were adults, and that's what adults usually do when they don't have the answer. They jerk each other around. I eventually solved the mystery by reading old books.

So as a teacher, you must understand that the adult technicians you're going to teach are probably going to make believe they understand things that they don't *actually* understand. They'll nod a lot.

And that's why it's so important for you to craft your lessons in such a way as to include *all* that stuff that people are afraid to ask. Don't assume they know even the most basic stuff. Take the time to spell it out. For many of the people in your audience, this will be the very first time anyone has done this for them.

And they will be very, very grateful. Their faces may not show this, but they *will* be grateful.

And you will have done your job.

Minutes. Ten minutes.

Do you remember the last James Bond movie you saw? The filmmakers didn't waste much time getting you totally involved in the action, did they? Nope, right up front, they hit you over the head with this big crazy chase scene – even before they played the opening credits! James Bond dispatched about 150 bad guys in those first ten minutes and blew up half of some foreign country. And you sat there on the edge of your seat, didn't you? *Sure* you did. So did I.

There's a reason why the filmmakers do this, you know. They want to grab you by your lapels and make sure you pay attention for the next couple of hours. They want to make sure they've got your undivided attention, and this is one of the reasons why they've managed to keep James Bond alive and well and making a gazillion bucks since 1962.

Bond. James Bond. He lets you know *right away* that he's going to be worth watching.

And you've got to do the same thing with the technicians you're trying to teach.

The way I figure it, when you stand up in front of *any* group of technicians you have about ten minutes to *prove* that you're worthy of their undivided attention. Most technicians will give you that much time, but if you don't grab them by the eleventh minute you might as well give up. They will have turned you off.

So how are you going to prove you're worth it – and quickly? What can you say that will get them as interested in *you* as they would be in a good movie?

Do one of the following things:

- Tell them something they most likely don't know.
- Show them something they've never seen before.
- Play a trick on them.

Let's look at these options one at a time.

Tell them something they most likely don't know.

I did a seminar once where the goal was to help a group of technicians get over the belief that the services their company offered were too expensive. Most of the technicians had the attitude that, "We're not going to offer *that*. It's *much* too expensive! No one will *ever* go for it." Since technicians can be the greatest salespeople a company has, this was obviously a bad attitude for them to have.

I *loved* the challenge this offered and I knew that I needed a story about the toughest sale ever made to convince these guys that what they faced wasn't really that difficult. I needed a story that captured the imagination. It also had to be a story that they had probably never heard.

I found just such a story in a book I had read about Canada. It was the story of Sir Sanford Fleming. Fleming was a railroad engineer who got it in his head that he could build a railroad that went from one side of Canada to the other. The challenge he faced, however, was that in the 1880s when he first got his idea, there were over 100 time zones in Canada. And people thought that this was God's will. You could travel as little as 40 miles and the time would change by several minutes.

Fleming knew that he'd never be able to build a railroad that spanned his country unless he first came up with a way to convince everyone in Canada (and throughout the rest of the civilized world) that they should change the way they perceived time.

Now, think about that for a moment. If I were to ask you to do that today, where would you begin? You have the advantage of the Internet, social networks, telephones and email, which Fleming didn't have. But where would you begin?

At that point in the story, the group I was teaching became very pensive. This was a story they had never heard. I had proposed a challenge they had never considered, and they sat there wondering what they would do if faced with such a challenge. It had nothing to do with the work they did. It was a mental exercise in salesmanship – a true story no less! – and they sat and considered it during those first critical ten minutes of my talk.

I went on to tell them of how Sir Sanford Fleming managed to change the way the world told time by creating Standard Time. People at first were *very* concerned because they weren't sure the cows would know when to make milk and the chickens to lay eggs, but as you know, everything worked out just fine.

And the technicians began to realize that if Sir Sanford Fleming could somehow convince the entire civilized world to change time itself, then they could probably convince people that *their* work was worthy of consideration – even if it *did* cost more than the competition's.

Those guys paid attention to what I had to say after that story because I had captured their imaginations within the first ten minutes.

You've only got ten minutes to *prove* it. Can you?

Show them something they've never seen before.

Here's a good example of what I'm talking about. People who work with heating systems look at gauges all the time. They're forever reading pressures and temperatures and trying their best to figure out what it all means when they're troubleshooting a system.

Someone once sent me a very peculiar gauge with a note that read, "Any idea what this is?" I had no idea, but I figured that someone else might know. I meet a *lot* of people in my travels. So I began to take the gauge with me to the seminars I was doing all around the country. I'd start the day by holding up the gauge and asking the same question the guy had asked me. "Any idea what this is?" I'd say.

I grabbed the technicians' attention immediately because the gauge had a single needle, but *two* scales. One read in "Atmospheres" and the other read in "Minutes." In case you don't know, one "Atmosphere" is equal to 14.7

pounds per square inch. This gauge went all the way up to 135 Atmospheres, which is nearly 2,000 pounds per square inch. That is a bodacious amount of pressure!

The weird thing about the gauge, however, was that the manufacturer had printed the "Minutes" scale both upside-down and as a mirror image. You had to hold the gauge in front of a mirror to read it. This scale went from 0-35 minutes, with a hand-drawn red line at 30 minutes. It seemed to warn, "Danger! Don't go over 30 minutes!" But 30 minutes of what? I had no idea.

On top of this, it was also *very* old.

So I'd stand there with this strange instrument and speculate on why someone might have needed such a gauge. In what industry or technical pursuit might you find the need to measure both pressure *and* time? And keep in mind that these two elements would have to tie together in some way because there was only *one* needle on the gauge. It was obviously measuring a change in pressure (rise or fall?) over time. But why?

And then there was the *big* question. Why was the "Minutes" scale both upside-down and a mirror image to the "Atmospheres" scale?

The technicians would sit there and stare at me in wonder. During the first break, they'd come up to the front and ask if they could see the gauge. I'd hand it to them and they'd scratch their heads.

I had their full attention right from the start because I had shown them something they had never seen before. They paid attention to me all day long because they figured I just might show them, and tell them, a few more things they didn't know.

And did I know what the gauge was for? Of course I did!

And am I going to tell you?

Not a chance.

And that brings us to your third option.

Trick 'em!

Why do you suppose magicians are so popular? They bring out the kid in most everyone, don't they? The audience watches and gets tricked. People say, "Ooo!" and "Ahhh!" and they speculate on how the magician did what he did – but most folks don't *really* want to know. That would spoil the magic!

There are loads of tricks you can play on a group of technicians (or on *any* audience). I played one on you in the last section. I told you about this strange gauge and I'll bet I got you wondering about it. I told you that I knew what it was and how it came to be.

But then I held back the answer.

I could probably hold your attention all day long if you were in my class and I kept segueing back to that mystifying gauge. I could get to a point where all I'd have to do would be to hold it up and smile. You'd be hanging on my every word, hoping that I'd spill the beans. If you got up to go to the bathroom, I might wait for you to return and then shout out, "Hey, you *missed* it! I revealed the mystery of the gauge to the rest of the group while you were gone. Too bad." I would, of course, have asked the rest of the group to go along with me when I did this.

They would. You *know* they would.

And that would drive you nuts, wouldn't it? It would also bring the rest of the group closer together – and closer to me.

At the end of the day, *maybe* I'd tell you all about the gauge – if everyone worked hard.

But then again, maybe I'd just keep it to myself.

That group would talk about me for a long time to come, right?

They'd *remember* that class, wouldn't they?

That's the point.

There are lots of tricks you can play. I'd sometimes start a seminar by turning on the overhead projector and using a marking pen to draw a small dot, right in the center of an otherwise clear slide. On the screen behind me there would be a bright light with a single black dot right in the middle. I would then ask my first question of the day.

"What do you see?" I'd say.

The technicians would sit there for a moment, not quite sure what to say, but everyone in that room would have his eyes glued to that single dot on the screen.

"What do you *see*?" I'd ask again, this time a bit more urgently.

"A dot," one guy would blurt.

"What do *you* see?" I'd ask, pointing at a technician on the other side of the room.

"A period," he might say.

"How about *you* over in the corner? What do *you* see?" I'd go around and around, asking the same question until the answers started to get creative.

"I see a lump of coal in a field of snow!"

"I see a black hole in a bowl of milk!"

Finally, I'd stop abruptly and shout out, "What was the *question*?"

Someone would say, "What do you *see*?"

"Right!" I'd say. "So why are you looking up *there*?" I'll point to the dot on the screen.

Huh?

"I asked, 'What do you *see*?' and you immediately looked up there! Why? Is that *all* you see? Don't you see the wall behind the screen? Don't you see the overhead projector? Don't you see me? And what about the person sitting next to you? Don't you see him? There's a chair right here. Don't you see it? Look at the ceiling? It's there! See it? And all this other stuff that's all around us? Why are you looking *here*?" I give the screen a good hard slap with the palm of my hand.

"Because you *told* us to?" one technician will always say.

"No, I did *not*! I just asked 'What do you *see*?' You guys decided to look up there. And *that's* the trouble with troubleshooting. Sometimes you'll make up your mind about what's wrong before you look at the whole picture. That's what keeps you from finding the answers. But you know what, guys? Today we're going to be looking at *big pictures*. And I need for you to see *everything*. I need for you to open your eyes to a wide world of possibilities, and I need for you to have fun while you're doing it. Okay? Can we have *fun* while we learn today?"

Technicians *love* that trick.

And they will pay attention to me for the rest of the day because I was able to put one over on them right up front. I did it within the first ten minutes. I'm worth watching after that.

Get it?

There's a world of puzzles, optical illusions, and magic tricks out there. Spend some time looking for this stuff and work it into the opening of your talks. Pay attention to the world around you. Life is *filled* with fascinating things to ponder. There are *no* boring subjects. There are only boring people.

Here, consider this. I found this in a history book.

How come the cold's on the right and the hot's on the left?

You use the sink, don't you? Hey, who doesn't? You want to wash up so you reach down with your right hand and turn on the cold water. You ever wonder why the cold's on the right and the hot's on the left?

That used to trouble me, but I have a *lot* of time on my hands so I did some research. Here's what I found out:

Back in the days before there was indoor plumbing people used to have to walk out to a well and dip a bucket on the end of a long rope down into the water. They'd then have to hump that heavy bucket of water back up to the house and heat some of it on the wood stove or the fireplace to make hot water. It was quite a chore.

As time went by, they brought the water indoors by way of pipes and a hand pump, which they installed next to the kitchen sink. They placed the hand pump on the right side of the sink because (you guessed it!) most people are right-handed.

When they eventually got around to bringing water mains into homes, they put the cold water faucet on the right for the same reason – most folks are right-handed. If these people wanted hot water, they *still* had to heat it on the stove or the fireplace because few homes had boilers or water heaters in those days.

Anyway, when the water heaters and boilers eventually arrived on the scene the plumbers had to put the hot water faucet on the *left* because the cold was already on the right.

Got all of that so far?

Wonderful!

Now, if the cold's on the right because most folks are right-handed, and the hot's on the left because that space happened to be available, how come the flusher on the toilet is on the left? If most people are right-handed, shouldn't the flusher be on the right?

Now, *there's* something to think about, eh?

Here's what I learned through my research:

The plumbers first started to install toilet bowls inside people's homes during a time when most folks were still sitting in outhouses. There's no plumbing in an outhouse – just a wooden seat, some corncobs or the old Sears catalog, and a very nasty hole in the ground. People did their business and got out of that stinking place as quickly as possible for reasons I'm sure you can well understand. They didn't hang out reading the Sears catalog. Nor did they stand up to take a gander at what Mother Nature had wrought. Nope, they just got up and got out.

When the plumbing moved indoors, folks were no more inclined to examine their droppings than they were in the days of the outhouse. They just wanted to flush and get the heck out of there. The early toilets had pull chains connected to overhead water tanks, not flushers, as we know them today. Since most folks are right-handed, and since they wanted to flush while still seated, the pull chain went on the right (which looks like the left when you're standing in front of it). Make sense? Another mystery solved!

But wait; there's more.

If the cold's on the right because most folks are right-handed, and if the flusher's on the right (even though it *seems* to be on the left) for the same reason, how do we then explain the urinal?

That flusher on the urinal is *definitely* on the left, isn't it?

How come?

Well, my research paid off once again. The flusher's on the left because most guys are right-handed, and that hand is busy shaking Mr. Johnson right now.

I *guarantee* that you will have the technicians' total attention by the time you finish this lesson in plumbing history and ergonomics.

One last trick?

I told you a story about Sir Sanford Fleming and how he created Standard Time and changed the way the entire world gets things done from moment to moment, right? Without Sir Sanford, trains would be crashing into each other. So would airplanes. You wouldn't get to work on time. You'd be fighting with your boss and with your spouse and you wouldn't know when your favorite TV show was going to start.

Time, as we know it today, came from the mind of a single man, and it's only been around since November 18, 1883.

Did you know that?

Something to think about, eh?

Here's something else to consider. The lines on the globe that denote the places where time changes start and end at the North and South Poles. As you travel toward the Poles, the lines get closer together, don't they? How do you suppose that affects the way the folks way up north or way down south perceive time? Does it make them live faster than, say, folks who live near the equator? It takes you a heck of a lot longer to cross a time zone at the equator than it does when you travel in the Yukon, doesn't it?

And if you keep traveling north, you'll eventually be standing on the North Pole, won't you? That's the place where all those lines meet.

So what time is it there?

And is it 12 hours later at the South Pole?

And how come you only get jet lag when you travel from east to west, or west to east? You don't get jet lag when you fly from north to south, or vice versa.

How come?

And if the world is turning from west to east, couldn't you just take off from New York City in a helicopter, hover for a few hours, and then land in San Francisco?

And if not, why not?

And why does it get *colder* when you climb a mountain? Shouldn't it get *hotter*? I mean, you're getting closer to the sun, aren't you?

So why does it get so cold?

If you're on an airplane and the flight attendant mentions that the pilot has pressurized the plane for the higher altitude, how come the potato chip bag they hand you for lunch is swollen? If the plane is pressurized, shouldn't the bag get smaller, instead of bigger? What's *that* all about?

There you go. Just a few of life's mysteries to ponder. Take your time.

And try opening your next meeting with one of these gems. See how the technicians hang on your every word for the rest of the day.

And don't give them the answers.

Oh, and if you don't know the answers, do some research.

Search vs. research

I was having dinner in Canada with some friends and we got to that point in the meal where the waitress asked about salad dressing. "What do you have?" one of the guys asked, and she recited the list like a prayer. "I'll have the balsamic vinaigrette," he said.

"That dressing played a huge role in Canadian history," I said.

"Really?"

"Yes, the French are foodies, as you probably know, and they love their salads. They used to use plain vinegar, or, as they say in France, vinaigrette, which is sort of like wine. The French also love their wine."

He was listening attentively, of course, because this is a mighty fine story, even though I was just making it all up as I went along.

"But they needed something to cut the pucker factor of the vinegar," I made that face, and continued lying like a cheap watch. "They needed balsamic, which is the perfect mellowing partner for vinaigrette." My other dinner companions, who were now hanging on my every word, all nodded. Balsamic gets a lot of respect no matter where it shows up because nobody really knows where it comes from. It's like capers.

"The problem, though," I lied, "is that there are no balsam trees in France. If you want balsam trees, you have to go to Canada. In Canada, you throw a rock, you hit a balsam tree. And that's why there are so many French people in Eastern Canada. They sailed over, got the balsamic from the balsam tree bark. Balsamic is dark, right? Just like tree bark. And once they got what they needed, they saw no reason to travel further west. The English took over the west. English people don't like balsamic vinaigrette."

One of our younger friends looked skeptical but I'm pretty good at holding a serious stare. Another friend got on his smart phone and Goggled balsam trees. He read a few words, looked at a couple of photos, passed the phone to our younger friend who saw for himself, smiled and said, "Wow, I never knew any of this. That's amazing!"

Behold the power of search. Oh, and of lies.

Have you noticed that when you ask someone a question nowadays (and this is especially true of younger people) the first thing they do is reach for their phones and Google for an answer. "What's the score of the game? How tall is the Empire State Building? How many Btus will that boiler put out?" Whatever the question, we have the entire world's knowledge in our pockets.

But what if the answer is wrong? Who puts all that stuff in there? You think all that stuff is correct? Hey, maybe it's me talking salad dressing in there. You never know.

I'm of an age where I remember library drawers organized by Melvil Dewey's Decimal System. If I wanted to learn about heating systems, or why they speak French in Eastern Canada, or what all this fuss was about Mr. Dickens or Mr. Hemingway, or whatever interested me, I went to the library and read whole books. It was the way people my age learned. I read and grew older and developed a certain amount of perspective and a large amount of imagination. I can now tell a good story because I've read lots of books from cover to cover. That's research. Research redirects you and forces you to learn big-picture stuff. Search just answers the immediate question. Research is oak. Search is veneer.

Toward the end of my teaching career I had to deal a lot with the veneer.

"Here's a good book for you to read," I'd say to a young technician.

"Can't you just answer my question? I don't want to learn the whole thing. I just want an answer to this question."

"But how will you learn to troubleshoot, to reason, to think critically and analytically unless you approach the whole subject? Unless you research."

"I don't have time for that. I just like to Google."

"But you're searching me, aren't you. I'm your mini-Google right now, aren't I?"

"I guess."

"What will you do when I'm dead?"

"I don't know (shrugs). Search someone else, I guess?"

Few technicians are reading whole books and doing deep research and gaining true knowledge these days. They're searching.

And what are they searching? They're searching the stuff that the researchers put there.

Push that thought forward a few generations. If few in your industry are doing research, what will be there to search in the future? You can't take out what others don't put in.

I think we're quickly heading toward a time when the people who work on equipment - both old and new - may not be able to solve the problems with those systems because, raised on search, they won't know how to think critically and analytically. There's no button for that on the smart phone.

They'll be parts replacers. And anyone can replace parts.

Some food thought for you, Teacher.

CHAPTER THREE
Logistics

How to get a big group settled down on time

Okay, let's say your trade association recruits you to do a seminar for a big group of technicians. They've asked you to do this because you are an expert in your field. You accept because you are flattered that they would ask the likes of you in the first place.

The next thing you know, you're in charge of the whole works. You're responsible not only for the content of your presentation, but also for the logistics of the meeting. You are . . . the Lonely Man.

Sound familiar?

Okay, here's what you have to do to make sure things go smoothly on the day of your meeting.

First, someone is going to have to get all those technicians into the room and settled down. You'll need a registration desk and a person to run it. This person should be someone who can remain calm because I can *assure* you that those technicians will show up in big bunches.

It's something that always makes me smile. They arrive in clown cars. You know the kind you see at the circus? Your registration person will be sitting there with nothing to do, and suddenly there will be 20 people on line, all wanting to know where the bathroom is, where the coffee's at, where they're allowed to smoke, and whether they'll get something free to take home with them.

The easiest way to keep the registration line moving is to send each technician a confirmation when they sign up to take your course. In my company, we used a paid invoice for this purpose. The bottom part of the invoice was a tear-off sheet that served as the technician's seminar ticket. We made sure everyone was registered in advance, and that they paid the fee. This kept things moving smoothly on the morning of the meeting because the registration person didn't have to collect money, make change, or deal with credit cards.

The ticket had the person's name and company printed on it. The ticket was really for the benefit of the registration person. He has a master list of who's coming. If the line was long, he could just grab the tickets and check the technician off the master list later on. From time to time, we'd get someone who was substituting for someone else. The registration person just had to ask that person to change the name on the ticket (he can make the change to the master list later on when things slowed down).

I've never found it necessary to have people sign in. Some companies insist on this to prove that the technician actually showed up, but to me, this is childish and the ticket serves the same purpose. I see no purpose in starting the day by implying that each technician needs to be monitored like some school kid. We're dealing with adults here, right?

If someone forgot his ticket, his name will still be on the master list. The registration person can just put a check mark on the master. The same goes for anyone whose name was misspelled on the ticket or on the master list. Have the registration person make the changes later on so that the trade organization can correct their database afterwards.

Name tags

Some people hate them; I happen to *love* them. If I had my way, everyone in the world would wear a name tag. There's nothing nicer than to be able to address someone by name when you're having a conversation. In a big group, it's very difficult to remember everyone's name, and the name tags lend a sense of friendliness right from the start. It's a good way to begin.

Prepare the name tags beforehand. The simple, stick-on ones work well and you can make them with a computer and a laser printer. In fact, the same software that generates your master list and invoice/tickets can also produce your name tags. If you decide on the stick-on type, bend the corners of each one so that they'll come off the sheet easily when the crowd arrives. That helps move things along. There's nothing funnier than watching a technician who could probably take apart and reassemble a nuclear warhead get defeated by the paper backing on a sticky name tag. Peel 'em back beforehand!

The name tags should have the person's name in large letters and their company affiliation in smaller letters below their name. Everyone likes to see their own name "in lights" and that's why the person's name belongs up top and in BIG PRINT. Put the focus on the *individual*, not on their company.

I once did a seminar for a public utility. They had about 200 technicians coming and they printed name tags for everyone. The most visible thing on those name tags was the name of the utility. It was in *huge* letters and it occupied the upper 75% of the name tags. Below, in the tiniest type I've ever seen, were the individual technicians' names. I had to squint and get within a foot of each guy's chest to figure out what his name was, but I could read the name of the utility from across the street.

This was a wonderful example of a corporate ego trip. They were beginning the day by not so subtly letting each technician know that the Utility was at least three times more important than each technician was. Great way to begin a relationship, don't you think?

So focus on the individual and then have the registration person lay out the name tags on the registration table in alphabetical order by the *technicians'* last names, not by their company affiliation. Remember that there may be more than one person coming from each company. If you set it up by company, you have to alphabetize twice – by company, and then by the individuals' names within that company group. Why make things more complicated than they have to be?

Set up the name tags so that they face toward the arriving technicians. That way they'll be able to pick up their own name tag. This saves the registration person time and effort. The technician will be able to spot his own name a lot faster than the registration person can. The technician sees that particular name a bit more often than the registration person does, right?

So now all the registration person has to do is ask for the ticket and tell the technician to "Please pick up a name tag." I once had a sleepy technician respond to this instruction by asking, "Uh, which one?" To which the registration person replied, "How about if you pick up the one with *your* name on it?"

If a technician doesn't have the ticket with him, there will still be a name tag for him. The registration person will simply check the technician off the master list and send him in the general direction of the coffeepot.

And bring along some extra name tags in case you've spelled someone's name wrong, or if someone is substituting for another person.

If you set all of this up properly, things will go very smoothly and *anyone* will be able to handle that registration desk. My seminar work took me all over the United States and to foreign lands, and when our company sponsored a seminar I'd usually be traveling alone so we would arranged to have a temporary worker (typically someone from Kelly Services) meet me on the morning of the seminar to handle the registration and to spend the day with me, just in case something went wrong. Because we had spent the time figuring out how to make it simple the Kelly temp could walk in, sit down, and handle the registration process *immediately.*

Simple *works.*

Hello!

If you're the speaker, I *strongly* suggest that you greet each of the technicians as they arrive. Stand between the registration table and wherever the coffee is located. Look each person in the eye, smile, extend your hand, and say something like, "Hi! I'm Dan Holohan (but please use your *own* name!). Thanks so much for coming. We're going to have a great time today. The coffee's right inside. If you need to use the bathroom, it's right over there. Grab a good seat up front, we're going to get started in just a little while. I *really* appreciate your coming."

The technician will be putting on his name tag at this point. Use his name when you talk to him.

Please don't neglect this part of the teaching process. A lot of speakers do. They feel as though they are some sort of royalty that should be kept hidden away until they are announced from on high. Don't get sucked into this sort of ego trip. Be humble. *Thank* the technicians for coming to listen to you. Spend a few minutes chatting with each one. When you begin your presentation, each of those technicians will have met you personally. You won't be a stranger to them. They'll pay closer attention *because you took the time to let them know that they are important to you.*

Which they are.

There will, of course, be people who arrive while you're chatting with another person. Make a note of where they sit and wander over to them before you start your talk to say, "How are you doing? Sorry I missed you when you came in." Introduce yourself and thank them for coming. Ask them if the temperature in the room is okay. Ask if their seat is comfortable. Can they see the screen from where they're sitting? Ask. Thank them again for coming. Tell them that you'll be starting in just a little while. Smile, and move on.

In other words, be a gracious host. These people are flattering you by their presence. *Never* forget that. They are the reason you're there.

Keep them occupied

If you're having a large meeting where people may not know each other, you might want to give them something to do while they're waiting for the meeting to begin. This could be something as simple as leaving a puzzle on their tables. If it's a good brainteaser, the technicians will work on it while they're waiting for you to begin. Tie the puzzle into the opening of your talk if you can. This isn't at all hard to do. Just use your imagination. Where do you get puzzles? The Internet!

I'd often project a photograph showing people from the turn of the century at work or at play. The technicians walk in, sit down, and wonder what that's all about up there on the screen. When I'd begin the seminar, I'd tell a story about the picture and the history it represents. I'd weave a good tale that will convince them that I'm going to be worth listening to for a whole day.

I'd often play a Three Stooges video first thing in the morning as they were arriving. The technicians walked in and up to saw Curly, Larry, and Moe wreaking havoc with Mrs. Hottentot's plumbing and heating. Years have gone by and many of my students still tell me how much they enjoyed that. To which I say, nyuck, nyuck, nyuck.

Old radio programs from the 1930s or a comedy tape (nothing nasty, though) also work well. Just be sure to work it into your opening remarks.

Use your imagination. What you're looking to avoid is that deadly silence that settles over a room filled with strangers in the half-hour or so before the seminar begins.

So now they're in the room and you're all ready to start.

But what *time* is it?

Timing is everything in life

When I worked for that manufacturers' rep, most of the employees started their day in the office at 9AM and stayed until 5 PM. When I decided to start doing seminars for the technicians who bought our stuff from the wholesalers, I figured that 9AM was a *terrific* time to begin. After all, that's when we started *our* workday.

We held the meetings in our office on Long Island, and someone would have to show up at 7:30 AM on the morning of the seminar to start the coffeepot. This responsibility usually fell on me, and I'd have to ask one of the people in management to rise early as well since I didn't have keys to the place or the burglar alarm code. Together, we'd grumble our way into the office, moaning about what an ungodly hour it was.

More often than not, the technicians were sitting in their trucks out there in our parking lot, waiting for us to open the door at 7:30 AM. They'd already had their breakfast, mowed the lawn, painted the house, worked three hours and now they were just about ready for lunch.

The point being, *your* sense of time may not be the same as *their* sense of time.

Try your best to work around *their* sense of time.

Everyone's at their best at different times of the day. Some of us are morning people; others should never be disturbed until after lunch. We all have what psychologists call "Circadian rhythms." There's a time and a place for everything. For instance, I walk five miles every day, but I feel best when I do it early in the morning, usually around 7 AM. For me, that's a Circadian rhythm. I'll also take a 20-minute nap whenever I can during the afternoon, usually at 2:30 or so. When I wake up I feel like a new man. I'm ready to work on into the evening. Circadian rhythms.

Think about your own body rhythms for a minute. When do you feel sharpest? When are you dragging? Do you try to do your best work around your Circadian rhythms? You should, if you can.

When you're deciding on a time to start a meeting, you should carefully consider what's the best time for the technicians. When do you think they'll be the most attentive? When will they start losing their edge and need a break or some food? This becomes a huge consideration if you're scheduling an evening meeting. The technicians have probably been up since dawn and they've been working hard all day. And now you want them to stick around for a few hours at dinnertime and pay close attention to what you have to say?

Lots of luck.

In my business, I often had large seminars at hotels. I had to balance the starting time of the meeting against the needs of the technicians, the location of the hotel (traffic patterns are important), and the Circadian rhythms of the hotel staff (yes, they *also* matter!). I've found that an 8 AM starting time worked well for just about everyone. And even at that, when I arrived in the room at 6:30 AM to get things set up, there were usually a couple of technicians sitting there, just waiting for the meeting to start. They're an hour and a half early, but they couldn't sleep.

Now, when I say 8 AM I want you to know that not *every* technician will see that as an invitation to show up an hour and a half early. A lot depends on those Circadian rhythms. Some are going to interpret 8 AM as 8:15 AM or 8:20 AM, or as soon as they finish that last cigarette, or whenever the heck they feel like showing up ("Whew, traffic's *tough* today!").

So now you have two choices:

1. You can issue a memo stating, YOU **MUST** BE ON TIME FOR THE MEETING UNDER PENALTY OF DEATH, DISMEMBERMENT, OR SUDDEN UNEMPLOYMENT (whichever comes first).

2. Or, you can announce the start of the meeting at an oddball time.

Trust me; you'll get better results if you choose the second option.

Instead of starting the meeting at 8 AM, announce that the meeting will start *promptly* at, say, 7:56 or 8:03 or some other screwy time. That starting time will jump off the memo, or paid invoice, or whatever other paperwork you send the technicians. It lets them know that you're serious about them being on time – and you won't have to treat them like schoolchildren (Option #1). It also lets the technicians know right up front that, as a teacher, you do things a bit *differently*. It piques their curiosity, and their interest in you as a person.

And they *will* show up on time.

Now, there is one rule you must obey if you're going to do this. If you announce an oddball starting time, *make sure you stick to it*. If you say you're starting at 7:59, wander up to the front of the room at 7:57 and stand there looking at your watch for two minutes. Then start talking. If you have a watch with an alarm, set it to go off at exactly 7:59. Or get yourself one of those old-fashioned, wind-up clocks with the big bells. When it goes off, you go on.

Don't worry if some of the people haven't shown up yet. Don't be concerned if some of the technicians are still getting their coffee. Just *start*. They will immediately go to their seats and pay attention.

But whatever you do, do *not* make the mistake of announcing that you will *end* the day at an oddball time. You have *nothing* to gain by doing this (they're already there!) and it puts unnecessary time pressure on you. If you say, for instance, that the meeting will conclude at precisely 3:57 PM, you will have a room filled with technicians who will be looking at their watches instead of listening to you for the last 20 minutes of your meeting.

Just say that you'll end at 4:00 PM, or whatever, and then do so. There's nothing worse than keeping them there past the time you've announced for the end of the seminar. If you keep yakking until 4:20 PM, know that you are cutting into *their* time and that they will resent you for that. If you're not able to end on time, you haven't prepared properly. If people still have questions at the end of the seminar, tell them you'll be happy to hang around and answer them personally. *But cut the rest of the group loose*.

More on that later.

Later in my career, we found that evening meetings also worked well. This followed the Great Recession when many companies had gotten lean as far as employees went. The owners didn't want training cutting into their people's work hours so we switched to evening and hoped the Circadian rhythms cooperated. For the most part, they did.

I came up with two, three-hour "stock" meetings: Classic Hydronics, and The Dead Men's Steam School. Each covered a lot of information in a short time, and we always sold them out. We'd start at 5 PM with a buffet dinner for the guys. I'd start talking at exactly 5:30. We'd take a 15-minute break at 7, and then I would go back to talking, making sure that I shut up at precisely 8:45.

It worked.

What about latecomers?

Hundreds of companies and associations hired me over the years to teach technicians. We always had an agreed-upon starting time. When I got hired, the folks in charge would often ask for my suggestions on the timing, and I'll give them some options. I was *really* flexible when it came to this. I'd work within *any* time frame a sponsor required, but I needed to know in advance what that time frame was. Once they told me, I'd plan the content of the seminar to fill that time. That's why we talked about it in advance. That's why we came to an agreement – in advance.

But here's what happened.

Let's say the sponsor and I agree that the meeting should start at 8 AM. Now, the guy in charge wants to introduce me so that he can say a few words about his company or association. I think that's great. He's the sponsor and he should get in a plug or two.

So I'd find this guy at about 7:55 AM and say, "You ready?" He'd look at his watch and then scurry out to the registration table. "Not everyone's here yet," he'd say. "Let's give 'em a few more minutes. The traffic must be heavy."

I'd check with the guy at 8:10 AM. He still wanted to wait for the latecomers.

I'd check with him again at 8:15 AM. He'd still be waiting. He'd be looking out the front door and down the road. He'd be running around the parking lot looking for latecomers. He'd be scurrying back to the registration table, wringing his hands. He'd be wondering if he should make some phone calls.

By 8:30 AM things were going downhill pretty quickly. The technicians who had the courtesy and good sense to show up on time were getting restless and annoyed, and who could blame them? And now my timing was completely thrown off. I'm flexible enough to recover, but there's *no way* those technicians were going to get the full lecture. I couldn't make up for that much lost time by talking faster – even though I'm from New York.

Now, think about this for a minute. The sponsor is penalizing the technicians who showed up on time because some of the people who are *supposed* to be there on time haven't arrived.

Is that fair?

I don't think so either.

And that's why I am a *huge* believer in starting on time. I think it shows respect for the technicians who got up early and made it to the seminar when they were supposed to be there. If I don't start on time, what does that say to those guys? Next time, maybe they'll take their sweet time arriving as well. "Hey, let's stop for coffee. They'll wait for us. They *always* wait."

Not *me*! Not if *I* can help it.

Have you ever been kept waiting in a doctor's office? You had an appointment, didn't you? You got there on time, right? But they made you wait an hour or more.

How did that make you feel?

Why start off your new relationship with these technicians on the wrong foot? *Respect* them. Their time is just as valuable as yours. Start on time.

As for the latecomers, make sure you set up the room so that they have to enter from the rear. You don't want them coming in from the front because that's where *you* are. It's very distracting to have latecomers crossing between you and the audience, muttering, "Sorry, sorry, sorry" as they go.

And please don't rag on the people who come late. Just get them seated as quickly as possible. There *are* legitimate reasons for being late. Remember before when I told you about how the town of Wilkes-Barre, Pennsylvania decided to pave the roads around the hotel where we were having our meeting? Just about *everyone* was late that day. These things happen. And then there was that hotel in Rhode Island where the contractor was jackhammering the parking garage (right under our meeting!). If people can't park, they're not going to be on time.

When the latecomers arrive, help them find a seat. Ask the other technicians who are already seated to raise their hands if there's an empty seat next to them. If you have a big group it's often difficult to see the available seats.

Chat it up a bit in a lighthearted way with the latecomers as they're getting seated. Try this:

"How's the traffic?"

"Late night, pal?"

"Do you have a note from your mother?"

"Hey! Go to the Principal's office, young man, and wait for me there!"

Chat it up like that and watch what happens. The more you chat at them, the faster they'll get into their seats. But keep it all light and fun; *don't* try to embarrass them. Just get them in and get them seated.

Don't get into the technical "meat" of your subject for the first 15 minutes or so of your seminar. You'll be using this time to set the mood and to get it through their heads that you're worth listening to, anyway. I've found that latecomers usually arrive within 15 minutes of the announced time. By holding back the serious technical stuff, you can ensure that they won't miss anything that will be beneficial to their jobs. Use that first 15 minutes to get to know each other.

And don't take their lateness personally. Most of the time, they have a legitimate reason. The important thing is they're there – and they're ready to listen to *you*.

So get talking!

CHAPTER FOUR
Let me hear your body talk

Yep, that's right! Yep, that's right!

I once knew a guy who had the most peculiar habit. He was widely considered to be an expert in his field and he did a lot of teaching. Here's what he did that was weird.

During the time that he was talking to the class he would emphatically nod his head up and down in a most furious way. He'd be giving us some interesting facts, and while he was at it, he'd nod like a bobble-head doll. If you were within 50 yards of this guy you'd start nodding too. You wouldn't be able to help yourself. I'm serious! It was the *strangest* thing. We'd spend most of the day listening and nodding in the affirmative. On some days, I'd actually go home with a stiff neck!

I once asked him if he was aware that he was doing that and he told me that he was. I asked him why he did it and he explained that it is *very* hard to disagree with someone when you are nodding your head yes.

Go ahead and try it.

Nod your head vigorously up and down and say the word, "No!"

Feels pretty weird, doesn't it? Now try it again, but this time say, "Yes!"

Feel better?

That's called body language, and psychologists have written many books on this subject. If I'm trying to tell you something new, and I'm nodding my head up and down while I'm telling it to you, you will be more inclined to believe me than you would be if I was shaking my head no, or if I was holding my head perfectly still. This was one of the things that made this guy such a great teacher. You couldn't help but agree with him. But you *really* had to pay attention to notice what he was doing to you.

It was subtle – as is *most* body language.

Like to know more? (I'm nodding like *crazy* right now).

Clothes make the man

I'm a big believer in dressing like your audience dresses. If I'm talking to technicians, I'm *not* going to wear a three-piece suit because they're not going to be dressed that way. They'll be in work clothes.

I had to learn this the hard way. When I worked for the manufacturers' rep, I had to wear a tie because my old bosses thought that ties projected a "professional image." I'd stand up there and talk and I thought I was doing okay, but I know now that I could have been doing much better.

Here's how I found out.

My old boss once sent most of the people in our company to a seminar called "Marketing by Objective." A fellow named Dr. Gunther Klaus was giving the seminar and we were in a hotel in New Jersey. I was very young and this was a big deal trip for me because we got to stay away from home overnight and there were three other rep firms involved. It was all very exciting. Big business stuff!

Anyway, we all got dressed up in our suits and wing tip shoes, making sure we were projecting that all-important "professional image." We got to the meeting room bright and early and got settled in. There must have been 80 of us in the audience. I sat there waiting for this great speaker, who had been touted to us for weeks.

Well, Dr. Klaus walks in, right on time, but he's not wearing a suit, nor is he projecting that "professional image." Nope, Dr. Klaus is wearing blue jeans, a blue denim work shirt, opened to the middle of his hairy chest, cowboy boots, and a wide belt with a big silver belt buckle. Around his neck, he has a thick gold chain with a pendant in the shape of the Superman logo. He stands up there and he looks at us like he *owns* us.

Which, at the time, I suppose he did.

"We're here today to talk about marketing . . . by *objective*!" he shouts at us in a thick German accent. He gives us a flashy smile and then holds us spellbound for six hours. I had never seen anything quite like it in all of my young life.

He made me want to be a teacher.

Now, what Dr. Klaus was wearing seems to go against what I told you a few minutes ago. Here we had a guy who *clearly* did not dress like his audience. But what his clothing was saying to us was that he was a man of the trenches. He was letting us know that in spite of his Ph.D., he knew his subject in a *very* hands-on way. He was not just some *theory* man; he knew the world better than we did. It was that incongruous mix of his reputation, his degrees, and his dress that was totally captivating. He was a warrior; we were wimps. You couldn't help but pay attention to this guy.

Not long after this seminar, the guy in charge of a local trade association asked me to speak at their monthly meeting. They played me up in their newsletter as someone who was up and coming in the industry and who knew his business. None of that was true, but it helped pump up the attendance. I decided to show up at the meeting in casual clothing instead of a suit. So did everyone else. I'm not even sure *why* I did this. It just felt right at the time.

Anyway, at the end of the meeting, one of the technicians grabs me on the side and says, "You know, Dan, you *really* know what you're talking about. You're not like those 'suits' they usually get to come here and talk to us. You've *been* there. You know what's what out there in the *real* world."

I never again wore a suit while talking to technicians. My casual clothing made me different. In some odd way, it brought me closer to them. I've learned that there will be a *strong* sense of white collar vs. blue collar when you put technicians, managers, and teachers together in the same room. If you appear to be casual in your dress (more blue-collar than white-collar), the technicians will be more receptive and more willing to believe what you have to tell them. And that's your goal, isn't it? To get them to believe you?

Lose the tie. Get a Superman shirt.

And please don't misunderstand me. I am *not* saying that dressing a certain way is a substitute for knowledge and preparation. *Nothing* can take the place of knowledge and preparation, but once you've made yourself smart, you *will* do better if you make yourself casual.

Then try this. When you're walking up to the front of the room to begin your talk, all eyes are going to be on you. If you're wearing a sport coat, take it off and lay it on the back of a chair. If you're wearing a long-sleeve shirt, roll up your sleeves. In other words, *do something overt that represents relaxation.* This will not only help *you* to relax, it will also put the technicians at ease. Encourage them to get comfortable while you're doing this. It works wonders.

I'll often stop during a lecture if I sense that the group is getting tense and ask them if they're comfortable. "Feel good?" I'll say. "You relaxed enough? Here, take off your shirt, if you feel like it."

That's always good for a chuckle.

"Loosen your belt; you're among friends. Whoa! Not *that* loose, buddy! We're not *that* friendly around here!"

That one usually gets you a belly laugh or two. Belly laughs also help people relax.

You want to work hard to make the environment relaxing and casual. Technicians will respond to that. And when they're relaxed, they're going to be more open to what you have to say.

You'll see.

Stand and move!

Do not, I repeat, do *not* sit down while you're giving your talk. Stand and move. It's a subtle thing, but it's *very* important. By you being physically higher, your audience will immediately recognize that you have the floor. Standing is one of the things that puts you in charge. You instinctively know what I'm talking about, don't you? Here, let's say you wanted to have a casual discussion with a group of technicians, rather than a lecture. Let's say you're all in a room where there's a conference table. You wouldn't stand while they were seated around that table, would you? No, you'd probably sit next to them, wouldn't you? It's a casual discussion.

Now, think about the shape of that table. If it's round, people will feel more equal than they would if the table was, say, rectangular. Picture a rectangular table. You're sitting at the head; they're around the sides. You're in charge, right? You're in the most powerful seat.

Now move around to the side of the table and let someone else sit at the head. Did you feel the power shift away from you and toward that person at the head? Spend a moment thinking about why that is.

Your position in a room has a lot to do with the way the group perceives you.

A perfectly square table is almost the same as a round table because there's no discernible "head." This would change if there were a big leather blotter with a gold pen and pencil set in front of one of those seats, wouldn't it? Whoever sits there would be in charge, right? Think about it. It's a subtle thing, but it's very important that you "feel" this.

Now, imagine you're sitting with the technicians at a round table, just having a discussion. Suddenly, you stand up while you continue to speak. Can you feel the dynamics in that room change?

Now imagine that you start to move around the round table while you're still talking. Sometimes you're in front of this guy; sometimes he has to turn a bit to see you.

Who's in charge now? You are, right?

Okay, now go sit down again at that round table and continue your discussion.

Did you feel the change in the room? Suddenly, everyone's on an equal footing again, aren't they? How come? It's because you are physically once again at their level. You've also conceded your power to move around at will. That makes a difference.

The right sort of body language puts you in charge of your meeting.

It works the other way too, so be careful.

Move, but don't pace

Now, when I say you should move around, I'm not talking about dancing on your toes or pacing like a caged beast. I've seen some teachers who looked like they were walking guard duty at a men's prison.

First off, if you're right-handed, stand to the right side of the screen (if you're using one). This would be from the students' perspective. I say this because when you point to something on the screen you're going to use your right hand. You won't have to turn your back on the technicians to do that. If you're on the other side of the screen and you're right handed, each time you point, you'll be turning your back. Not good.

It's a little thing, but it really matters.

And don't move too much. If you do, you'll be distracting them from what you're saying. It's better to move forward and back than it is to move side to side. Step forward to reinforce a point, and them work your way back to where you were. There's less chance you'll be blocking their view of the screen that way.

Here, let me tell you a story about a teacher who sat too long. I have a buddy who went to a fancy college back in the Seventies. He told me about a course that he took in a lecture hall where the professor *insisted* on sitting on top of his desk over in the corner of the room near the window. One day the class got together before the professor arrived and decided to try to move this guy off his desk. They did this in a *very* simple way.

They all stared intently at the *opposite* corner of the room. This, of course, was body language.

Now, try to imagine what it must have felt like to be that professor. You're up there in front of the room, talking to about 50 students. You're perched on your desk by the window, as usual, *but your audience is turned toward the other side of the room.*

What are you going to do?

You're going to look over at that corner, too, aren't you?

Sure you are!

And when your entire audience *persists* in staring over there at what appears to be absolutely *nothing* but the opposite corner, what do you suppose you'll do sooner or later?

You're going to get up off your butt and move over to the place where they're staring, aren't you?

Sure you are. It's just human nature. Everyone wants to be looked at when they're speaking. It's part of how we validate our existence. *No one* likes to be ignored. And that feeling is even *stronger* when you're a teacher.

So the professor got up and moved.

And do you know what those students did as soon as he moved? They turned in unison and stared at his empty desk.

So of course he moved back.

And then they turned as a body to stare at the other side again.

They made the man crazy by the end of the semester.

And in case you were wondering, it was a course in *psychology*. The guy should have known better, right?

Fancy footwork

So you see a couple of technicians who are talking to each other during your lecture. Move toward them and watch how they stop chattering. If they *don't* stop chattering, pull up a chair right next to them and join in the conversation. "So what's the topic? Something unclear? Need help?" They'll stop talking to each other. Guaranteed.

Move toward any sleepers who seem like their heads are about to snap off their necks. Raise the volume of your voice as you do this. Watch how they wake up as you get closer. Smile down on them. Ask if they'd like anything. Coffee? Red Bull?

You stab your arm out to one side and point at that side of the room while you're telling a story. "Oh, the customer was coming down the driveway!" The technicians will turn to look at where you're pointing. You take one step in that direction. Pretend you're meeting the customer as he's coming down the driveway. Shake his invisible hand. Throw your arm around his invisible shoulder. Walk him back one step to where you started. They'll follow your every move and you're not even moving that far.

Get it? There's a *point* to this movement. If you're just pacing back and forth to give your audience a moving target they're going to get bored with you pretty quickly. *Move*, but move with *purpose*.

Move into the crowd to shake the hand of someone who answers a question correctly. This is a *very* powerful thing to do in a group setting. You're singling out one individual who has had the courage to speak up. You're shaking that person's hand or patting him on the back and making him feel like a superstar for a moment. "I wish I had a roomful of guys like *this* guy!" you shout.

Give the guy a lollipop if you have one.

And then go back to where you were.

Now pay close attention to this next one because this one is ridiculously subtle. When someone in your audience asks you a question, *immediately take a step **away** from that person*. If you take a step *toward* the person (which is a natural reaction) you are indicating to the audience that you are about to have a one-on-one conversation with the guy who asked the question. The audience will figure that it's time for them to take a mental break. After all, you're busy talking to *that* guy, right? You walked over to *him*, didn't you? You're answering *his* question, aren't you?

What does that have to do with *them*?

But watch this. When you take a step *away* from the person who asked the question, you are stepping **toward** the group. You're including them in the process. Again, it's a subtle thing, but your movement indicates that you have joined the rest of the group, *and as a group you'll now consider the guy's question*.

It's also important that you rephrase the question as you take that one step away from the questioner. By rephrasing the question, you're shifting the emphasis away from him and back toward the group. This makes it seem as though the entire group is answering the guy's question rather than just you. Now everyone is engaged in that question.

Try it once and you'll "feel" what I mean. (I'll tell you more about this technique later on.)

Soup for you!

Do you remember when Al Gore first ran for President? Remember how much abuse he took because he was so wooden? What made him that way? Was he nervous? Was he just *built* that way?

How do *you* look when you're up in front of a group? Do you look like Al Gore? Do you just stand there with your arms at your sides? Do you move your head? Have you ever given it any thought? Have you ever watched yourself on videotape?

You should.

I once worked with a guy who had to give a speech. This was his first time on the barrel and he was as nervous as anyone I had ever worked with. He was *more* than qualified to give that talk. He was well educated and had all sorts of real world experience. He knew his products, and he knew his audience.

I helped him put his outline together and then I had him rehearse the speech for me a few times. He stood there with his arms stuck to his sides. He kept his palms pressed tightly against the outsides of his thighs. He looked like he was about to be fired from a cannon.

"Can you move your arms a bit?" I suggested.

"I *am* moving them," he said, squeezing them even tighter to his thighs. It looked like his cuffs were stitched to his pockets with rawhide.

"You're *moving*?" I asked.

"I think so," he said. I'm telling you, he was the original Cannon Boy.

We were in my house so I went to the kitchen and brought back two cans of Progresso minestrone soup. The soup wasn't for lunch, though.

"Hold these," I said. He looked at me as though I was nuts. I pried his hands off his thighs and put a big can of soup in each one.

"Why do I have to hold *soup*?" he said.

"It's not just soup," I said. "It's *minestrone* soup. And it's to remind you that you have *hands*, and that those hands are attached to *arms*. And that those arms can be beautiful if you let them fly freely. Like big eagle wings."

"Eagle wings?" he said.

"Yes!" I said. "You ever see an eagle in flight?" I held out my arms and waved them with grace.

"Eagles *soar*," I said.

We went through his speech about 50 times more, but this time with the minestrone soup. I wouldn't let him put down those heavy cans until he figured out that he had arms. I made him hold the soup for the rest of the day. After a while, he began to move his arms a bit because soup cans get heavy after a few hours and there's just so much time you can spend gripping them before you're *compelled* to turn your palms upward.

He did.

A while after that, he actually began to lift his arms up and down and gesture with the cans. He did this to keep the blood moving.

When I finally took the soup cans away from him, he was doing a nice job of flailing his arms quite freely. Just like an eagle lifting off the ground. He was relieved to be rid of all of that minestrone weight, and that set his arms free. He looked *much* more natural, and he was even *more* relaxed knowing that he wouldn't have to hold the soup during his actual talk.

He soared like an eagle during that talk. I was there in the audience, and I was proud of him.

You know, one of the things you'll realize when you're watching a videotape of your speech is that you have to *really* exaggerate your movements to make them look natural. It's almost like acting. What feels to you like a broad, sweeping movement of your arm looks to your audience like a simple and casual gesture. You have to watch a videotape of yourself to fully understand this.

So have someone videotape you sometime while you're giving a talk and then sit and watch yourself for a while. It *really* helps. You have to *exaggerate* to look natural.

Strange but true.

Loud and clear?

When I took the Dale Carnegie Course they put us through an exercise one night that I will *never* forget. The purpose of the exercise was twofold: to help us get over the fear of looking silly in front of a crowd, and to help us speak as clearly as possible.

Try this. Take your tongue and tuck the end of it between your lower lip and your teeth. Got it? Great!

Now start reading this book out loud. Start right now. Go ahead. No one's around to see how dumb you look. At Dale Carnegie we had to say things like, "My brother Reginald lives in Rhode Island."

Go ahead. Say it.

How does that sound?

Pretty silly, eh?

Try doing it in front of a live audience some time.

You will *quickly* get over your fear of looking silly.

Try talking with your tongue in that position for 15 minutes or so. Then put your tongue back in your mouth and speak normally. Do you hear how much clearer you sound now that you have an increased awareness of your tongue?

It's feels almost as good as it does when you finally put the soup cans down.

Word whiskers

Another thing you need to be conscious of are word whiskers. These are those extra words that grow on our sentences. Most of the time, we're not even aware that they're there.

Years ago, I took our twin daughters to Washington DC to look at Georgetown University. An incredibly intelligent young woman named Marie took us on a tour of the place. She was going to be a senior in the fall and she knew her university well. She pointed out all the features and benefits of the place as we trudged along in the doughy July heat and humidity. After about 15 minutes I began to realize that, according to Marie, Georgetown was *VERY exciting!* I say this because after describing each event, building, course in the curriculum, athletic field, upcoming nationally known speaker, dormitory room, marble statue, meal in the cafeteria, monument, and drinking fountain, she would shake her mane of curly hair and giggle, "It's *VERY exciting!*"

And it was *VERY exciting*. For about five minutes. After that, it became *VERY distracting!* I found myself keeping track of how many times she repeated this phrase and I lost count (and nearly lost my mind) after she had said it 147 times.

That's a word whisker.

I had a professor in college who would say "if you will" after every other sentence. "The test, *if you will*, will be on Friday, *if you will*." This woman nearly drove an entire class over the edge with what I came to think of as a World Class Word Whisker, if you will. The only way we managed to make it through the semester was to start a lottery. We'd each put a quarter in a cup on our way into class, if you will. Then we'd take a guess at how many times she'd use that evil phrase. We had three official counters, if you will, and we'd average their results at the end of each session. Whichever suffering student came closest won the pot. True story.

When our eldest daughter, Kelly, was 15 years old I used to bet her friend, Diana, ten bucks that she could not talk to me for five continuous minutes without saying the word "like." She took me up on it at least two dozen times and was *never* able to win the money. She'd start by saying, "I know I can, like, *do* this!" And that would be the end of that.

Teenagers are, *like* . . . like that, ya know?

And speaking of "ya know," that's another one that can drive you crazy once you start hearing it, *ya know*?

And then there's the ever-popular "Um." The next thing we're going to talk about, um, is the framus and, um, how it fits into the Farquar flange, which is, um, over here. Ya know?

It's, like, *maddening*!

And how about the word whisker that makes you sound weak? Many young people do this. They turn each sentence they say into a question by going up an octave on the last word. Like this:

"I was on a *job?* And I took out my *tools?* And I fixed the *problem?*"

Can you hear the weakness in that? It's as if the speaker needs your approval at the end of each sentence before he can move on to the next one. If you're a teacher and you do that, technicians are going to think you're uncertain about everything. And if they think that, they're not going to listen to you.

So please *listen* to yourself when you're speaking. Pay close attention to what you're saying. If you have any word whiskers try your best to shave them so that they don't distract your audience from hearing your message. Ask a loved one to point them out to you. If you have kids, ask them to raise their hands every time you sprout a word whisker. They'll drive you crazy, but they'll, like, help you get rid of them once and for all, um, ya know?

And besides, you don't want, like, a classroom full of technicians running a lottery around your speech habits, do you?

Huh?

Regional accents and speech patterns

I'm from a place called Long Island, which is a small nation off the East Coast of New York City. Rosetta Stone sells a four-level program for our language. We don't call it

Long Island in the American English sense. We say Lawn Guyland.

Ya know?

"My doughta? Huh and me went to da stour to get food for the dowg and some bottled wawda."

It's like that.

When I traveled to other parts of the country I had to grapple my Lawn Guyland accent into submission. If I don't, the technicians in the audience would spend much of their time giggling at me.

I mentioned that my specialty is heating. Well, on Lawn Guyland we pronounce the word "radiator" with a short-a so that it rhymes with "gladiator." Technicians roll in the aisles when that one gets loose.

I try my best not to let it loose.

We also shorten "soda pop" to "soda." If I'm in the Midwest and I say "soda" the whole room cracks up because those folks say "pop." To them, "soda" is seltzer. To me, "pop" is somebody's father.

So there.

In California, on the other hand, you order neither soda, nor pop, nor soda pop. You order "coke." You walk into a restaurant and say, "I'd like a coke," and the waiter smiles and says, "What flavor?" You say, "Orange," and that's what you get.

Coke is generic for soda (pop?) in California.

Go figure.

Once while in Denver, Colorado, I mentioned to a group of technicians that I kept a pen and a pad on my nightstand. I did this, I explained, so that if I woke in the middle of the night with a good idea, I would have a place to write it down before it flew out of my sleepy skull.

During the break, one of the technicians approached me and asked, "Dan, what's a *pad*?" I was flabbergasted. "It's a . . ." I looked around the table and spotted a yellow stack of bound, lined paper. I picked it up and said, "*This* is a pad."

"Oh!" he said. "You meant a *tablet*."

"You don't say the word 'pad' in Denver?" I asked.

"Sure we do," he said. "But to us, a 'pad' is a big cement base that we pour on a job site to hold up a big pump. We were just wondering why you had a *pad* on your nightstand, is all."

See how tough it is to be understood if you're more than 50 miles from home?

The best way to get around this challenge if you're a Traveling Teacher of Technicians is to listen very carefully while you're in an area. If you're in a restaurant for breakfast, sit near people who are chatting so that you can listen to the way they speak. Try to pick up on any regionalisms they use and work them into your talk. For instance, I was once explaining a fine point of steam heating to a technician from Richmond, Virginia. His eyes lit up when he finally understood and he said, "I git it! You cain't start a diesel in fourth gear, right?"

That's a regionalism.

And I'm sure it made *perfectly* good sense to him and his buddies.

Ya know?

You will probably *never* sound like a TV newsreader, but you should strive to get rid of any pattern in your speech that draws attention away from your message. If you find this to be absolutely impossible, then use your accent to your best advantage. For instance, I might work my Lawn Guyland accent into a story about a bunch of rude New Yawkas, ya know? Technicians from other parts of the country actually think New Yawkas are *rude*. But ay! Wadda dey know?

Now get outta my way, jerky. I gotta move on!

Put your HANDS on the television!

I can spend *hours* watching the preachers on TV. I'm not about to send them a personal check, mind you, but I *love* to watch them do the thing they do. I would encourage you to check them out as well. Listen to the way they use their voices. Watch how they move around the stage and command it. Notice how they use gestures to punctuate and emphasize their message. These folks are *good* and you can learn a lot from them.

After you've worked your way through a bunch of preachers, start on the politicians. Watch what they do with their hands. Watch the way Bill Clinton gestures while he's making a point. He positions his right hand as though he were holding a pen and he beats a tattoo with it to punctuate his words and to add a rhythm to his speech. Hillary did the same thing, only not as successfully.

Note the way Bill averts his eyes downward in a most humble way, and then looks up to the camera again with that big "Ah shucks!" grin of his. Love him or hate him, he is *masterful* at what he does, as was Ronald Reagan. The two have very similar gestures when it comes to the "Ah shucks!" thing. And they're both very similar to John F. Kennedy when it comes to being emphatic and convincing. Check out the old film footage. And watch Bobby Kennedy while you're at it. Compare him to LBJ.

And don't miss what Donald Trump does with his right hand. It's continuously in motion. He goes from the okay sign, to an open palm, held forward (STOP!), to an extended pointer and thumb (other fingers folded). This intentionally or not, forms a big letter L. He then goes back to the okay sign. It's fascinating to watch and very powerful.

Watch Martin Luther King and study him as he delivers his famous speeches (especially the "I have a dream" speech). Focus on the pacing and the changes in volume that he used so effectively. Listen, too, to Winston Churchill and FDR and Huey Long and any other great orator you can get your hands on. Forget about *what* they're saying for a moment and just pay attention to *how* they're saying it. Focus on their gestures and their speech patterns. There's *so much* you can learn simply by watching them all.

Learn from them.

Audiotape your seminar and listen to yourself talk as you drive around town. Listen for your own inflections, pacing, volume changes, and enthusiasm. Can you "hear" yourself smiling? Do you find yourself interesting? Would you want to spend a full day listening to the likes of *you*?

Be highly critical of your performance. It hurts, I know, *but this is the only way you're going to get better at it.*

Listen to audio books while you're driving. Audible.com hires some of the best readers in the world. Listen to the way these masters use their voices to enhance the stories the authors have penned. Give it a try. It's a great use of that time you spend staring at your windshield.

CHAPTER FIVE
How to tell a story

Aloha!

I got hired four times to teach a seminar about steam heating in Hawaii.

Pretty cool, eh?

The first group that hired me was from Alaska and they were there on a convention. We had a ball. While I was flying there from New York City with my wife, The Lovely Marianne, a thought occurred to me. There are only *three* possible ways you can get to Hawaii. That, to me, seemed so *very* profound at the time. Hey, it's a long flight.

I leaned over to my sweet wife and whispered in her ear, "You know there are only *three* ways you can get to Hawaii."

She stared at me for a moment and then said, "What's your point?"

"Well," I whispered, "can you *name* them?"

Now, you should know up front that this sort of game drives The Lovely Marianne crazy, which is why I was doing it. As I said, it was a long plane ride and I needed some marital amusement.

"Leave me alone," she said, turning back to her book.

Which I did.

About ten minutes passed and she turned to me, as I knew she would. "What's the third way?" she asked.

"Excuse me?" I said.

"What's the *third* way?"

"The third way to do what?" I asked.

"To get to Hawaii," she said. "You can go by *air*. You can go by *sea*. What's the *third* way?"

"Don't you know?" I said. "Can't you figure it out? It's so *simple* if you just think about it."

She scowled at me and went back to reading her book – for a while.

General Hospital

I worked from home for many years, which is also pretty cool. At one point, I have the responsibility of setting the VCR each afternoon at 3:00 PM to tape the soap opera, *General Hospital*. When my daughters got home from school they'd say hello, give me a kiss on the cheek, and then ask the inevitable, "Did you tape *General*?" I'd nod and smile and they'd head right for the TV. This went on for a bunch of years.

Our four daughters, and millions of other Americans, were hooked on that show, and had been for a long time. I figure there's a lesson there. Most people *love* a good story, and the longer the story runs, the more the people seem to like it. This is why shows such as 24, Homeland, The Wire, and House of Cards are so popular. And it's nothing new. We used to speculate about who shot J.R. Ewing. And years and years before that shooting, folks would flock to go to the movies every Saturday afternoon to find out if Pauline made it through her perils. After all, wasn't she on a buzz saw last week? And how will she ever get off of those train tracks?

People *love* a good story!

That's why there are so many stories in the Bible.

That's why Jesus taught in parables.

People love stories. They *remember* stories. They *respond* to stories. They sit up and pay attention to stories. And that's what you're looking to do with the technicians you teach, isn't it? Don't you want them to sit up and pay attention?

So tell 'em a story!

The best stories spring from your own experience, from what you do from day to day. You may think your life is dull but, believe me, it's *not*. If you're not seeing the powerful lessons in the simple things around you then you're just not paying attention. There are *no* boring subjects in this world. There are only boring people.

Refuse to be one of them.

Consider this story, for example. It sprang from my imagination as I stared at this small copper fitting I have kept on my desk for nearly 50 years.

A simple copper elbow

When I was 20 years old I took a job working for a manufacturers' rep. I told you about this earlier, but what I didn't tell you was that my father was my immediate boss. He didn't own the company, though; he was just an employee like me. And since we were the first father/son combination ever to show up at this company he was especially hard on me. He didn't want anyone to think I was being favored. We were the representatives for the Northern Indiana Brass Company at the time. NIBCO makes copper fittings to connect plumbing and heating pipes but we didn't stock any of them. The factory would ship the goods directly to the wholesalers and my job was to keep track of who got what. I was a clerk. From nine until five I would look at factory-shipment records and make check marks on the customers' orders. I sat at an old wooden desk and shuffled paper all day long. I had a mechanical calculator that was the size of a toaster oven. It chugged back and forth like an unbalanced washing machine. Day after day, I processed paper, never really knowing what I was dealing with. I never got to meet the people who made, or bought, or installed the products we sold.

One day I wandered out to the warehouse where the company kept a very small supply of copper fittings, which we used mostly for samples. I picked up a simple copper elbow and carried it back to my desk. I liked the way it blinked brown and shiny in the fluorescent light. That afternoon when the phone calls died down I found myself playing absentmindedly with that copper elbow. I stuck my pinkie through it and felt its smoothness. I remember wondering how they got it to be that smooth. I had never been to a factory. I could only wonder.

In the days that followed, and mostly out of boredom, I began to think more and more about that simple copper elbow. I picked it up and held it to my nose. Copper has a particular odor that's unlike anything else. It reminded me of the taste I'd get in my mouth when I ran too hard on autumn days during touch football games. That simple copper elbow reminded me of friends who had moved away years before.

As the days went by I started to think about where the copper came from. I imagined a mine in Chile or some other exotic place I would probably never get to visit. Chile was in the news a lot back then and I read that they had copper. I thought of the men who went down into the earth and clawed the copper from the rocks. I imagined their skin to be as brown as the copper itself. I wondered what their lives were like, if they had wives and children, and if their children would someday also work in the mines.

I began to think about the ore and how the copper got from the mines to the smelters and then (in what form?) to the factory in Elkhart, Indiana. I thought of the ships that must carry the ore northward, and the men who piloted those ships. I wondered if they got bored staring at the sea and their instruments day after day. I thought of these things as I made my check marks on the customers' orders. One hundred #607 elbows shipped, size: half-inch. Two hundred #611 copper-by-copper tees, size: three-quarter inch. I checked them all, and wondered if this was how my life was to be.

When the copper got to Elkhart it had to be unloaded, and someone must be doing that hard work right now I imagined. I tried to picture what those men looked like. How big were their arms? Did they stop on their way home and drink beer and complain about the boss while their wives waited for them with crying children? I figured these men had much in common with the men who mined the copper. I tried to imagine them meeting in some roadhouse on a gray Midwestern afternoon. Would they recognize each other?

I thought about the machines at the factory that were powerful enough to bash copper into the shape of an elbow, or a tee, or a threaded union. How much force would it take to do that? And what would it sound like? And who invented and built that machine? And what did it weigh? And who figured all of this out on paper?

I closed my eyes and tried to imagine what it must be like to go to work in that factory day after day, knowing you would probably be doing this for the rest of your life. I imagined what it might feel like to be a former, small-town football hero who has now grown a potbelly. He does this work every day in the Heartland of America. The crowds no longer cheer. He has only the pounding of the machinery, and that pounding is relentless.

And then I thought of the constant buzzing of the semi's wheels as it races along Interstate 80 on its way to New York City with the copper fittings. The driver stares as far as his headlights will allow through a bug-splattered windshield. He smokes an unfiltered cigarette, and a country song plays softly on the radio. An old dog sleeps on the torn passenger seat. The driver stubs out the butt, and then lights another as the miles fly out from under his heavy truck. He thinks about his wife, who is as far away as next week.

And in New York City a few months later, a young man with long hair drives a forklift onto the back of another truck and unloads the fittings into his boss's warehouse. He has a date that night with a girl he will someday marry. He's not thinking about the copper, only about the girl.

The fittings sit on the wholesaler's shelf for a while and quietly gather dust. One day a heating contractor picks up a heavy cardboard box filled with fittings and a half-dozen other items and tosses it all into the back of his old van. He goes from job to job, making repairs and installing new equipment, and on one Tuesday morning, he reaches into the box and comes out with a simple copper elbow. He cleans the inside of the fitting with a stiff wire brush, swabs some flux over it, and slips it onto the end of a bright copper tube. He never stops to think of how precise the fit is. He never considers what has gone into the mating of fitting and tube. People working all over the world have played a part in this precision, but none of them give much thought to the mating either. They all just go to work every day and do their repetitive tasks. Just like me. We will never meet.

The contractor touches a spark to the end of his torch and watches the fire pop to life. He holds the flame to the base of the fitting and waits. The gas, which once slept deep in the earth, kisses the copper in a way that seems as old as creation.

When he has finished his work, the contractor lets hot water surge through the tubing and around that simple copper elbow. He packs up his tools and walks out to his truck. He's going to take his young son to a basketball game that night.

That evening, the homeowner sits and reads his newspaper in a warm living room. His wife watches television and his children do their homework. The man casually flips past a small article about trouble in a copper mine somewhere in Chile, a country that is too far away to concern him. He wets his fingertip and flips the page.

Do you understand? Do you see? There are *no* boring subjects. There are only boring people who can't tell a story because they're not paying close enough attention to the magnificent world around them.

Refuse to be one of them.

Aloha again!

I had finished giving my talk to the Alaskans there on the beautiful Kona coast of the big island of Hawaii and we had the rest of the afternoon to ourselves. The Lovely Marianne and I decided to hang out by the beach. We were sitting on a couple of chaise lounges and she was sipping an umbrella drink. I was sucking down a big cold beer.

"So what the hell is the third way?" she asked, clearly annoyed.

"Third way?" I asked. "What third way, my little tropical flower?"

"To *get* here?" she shouted.

"To the beach?"

"No, you evil monster! To *Hawaii*! You can go by *air*. You can go by *sea*! What's the third way you can get there?"

"Get *here*?" I asked, quite innocently.

"*Yes!* If you don't tell me, I'm going to lose my mind."

"Oh look!" I said, pointing out toward the cobalt blue Pacific. "Is that a whale?"

Oh, I almost forgot!

Be natural when you're telling a story. Make believe you're sitting around having dinner with a couple of good friends. Lay out all the details. Say the character's names and tell a bit about them. What do they look like? Do they have a peculiar odor? How are they dressed? All these details will add to your tale, giving it depth and making it more interesting. Remember, you want your audience to be hanging onto your every word, and you do that by spelling out the details.

Add color to your story by using colorful speech. A woman can jump out of her chair . . . or she can spring up like a ballerina in a music box. A man can be overweight . . . or he can look like the Country Buffet Poster Boy.

Do you see the difference? This is what I mean when I say you should add color.

The pipe can be hot . . . or it can be several degrees hotter than Hell.

The day can be cold . . . or it can be colder than outer space.

The man can be big . . . or he can fill the doorway with his hugeness.

The woman can be good looking . . . or she can make angels jealous when she smiles.

Use your imagination. And use colorful descriptions.

Gesture wildly if the story calls for it. If I were telling you the story about The Lovely Marianne sitting on that beach in Hawaii, I'd be waving my fist and scrunching up my face and looking as frustrated as she was on that gorgeous day when the warmth of the sun flowed like honey over her tanned body (see the colors?). Gestures make the story even *more* real. They draw your audience into the action. Take advantage of them. Let your body talk.

Change the tone, pitch, and volume of your voice as you tell your tales. Tone is the inflection you put into a sentence.

I *like* you!

I like *you*?

Can you hear the difference?

Pitch is a change in the highness or lowness of a sound. Let's say you're a man and you're telling a story about a woman. If you imitate her voice, you'll change the pitch to make it higher. You'll lower the pitch to go back to your man's voice. If you listen to audio books, you'll see example after example of this as the readers change the pitch of their voices with each character. After a while, it feels like there's a whole cast of characters on the tape rather than just one person creating the many voices.

Volume is the audible level of your voice. Whisper when necessary. Shout or scream if the story calls for it. Use volume to wake up anyone who may be dozing off.

Imitate those people in your story. Stand the way an old man might stand. Crouch down or get on your knees behind a table and raise the pitch of your voice if you're telling a story about a little kid. This will captivate your audience. They don't expect this from a teacher.

Rent any movie staring Robin Williams (especially *Dead Poets Society*) and study his incredible animation. Then do the same with Jim Carrey.

Make yourself the brunt of your stories if it's appropriate. This will make you more human and bring you closer to the technicians you're trying to teach. This works *especially* well if you're telling the story about a younger you (I've done this several times already in this book). People consider me to be an expert in steam heating, but years ago I was on a job with a technician who asked me where to put the boiler. I chose a suitable spot in the basement. We moved the boiler into place, and the basement floor opened up and swallowed the boiler, the technician and me. It wasn't my finest hour, but it makes for a great story (and I just made myself the brunt of it again!).

After that happened, I wrote this long poem in its honor. I memorized it and would start each of my steam seminars with it. It certainly got the technicians' attention.

Dangerous Dan and The Hole in the Ground

I'll tell you a tale that will keep you spellbound,
Of Dangerous Dan and the Hole in the Ground.

It started out simply on a day just like this,
At a steam seminar I wanted no one to miss,

Especially Pete, who was a plumber by day,
And who wanted to come but his boss said, "No way!"

But I wanted him there for this was Pete's dream.
You see, the plumber by day was a student of steam.

And at night he would sit 'til the first crack of dawn,
With the books and the drawings of a Day Long Gone.

And he studied the steam and the work of Dead Men,
Who had come years before and who weren't there then

To teach him the art he so wanted to know,
So when he heard of this class, well, he just had to go.

So I took up his fight and I spoke to Pete's boss.

I said, "Look at this day as a gain, not a loss.

"How valuable Pete will be after that day!"

And Pete's boss relented, and he said "Okay."

"But have him back Friday or you'll take the heat.

I've a steam job to do, and for that, I need Pete."

"He's the only one here who can or ever would

Tackle the steam. The others are no good."

"Sure they know hot-water, leaky pipes and clogged drains,

But for them, steam has always been too much of a strain."

So I promised sincerely that I'd have Pete back there,

But what I didn't count on was Pete's glassy stare.

Like a small kid at Christmas Pete was at our place,

And I should have known then by the look on his face,

That the very next morning, not giving a whit,
Pete would call up his boss and just simply. . . quit.

"I'm striking out on my *own!*" Pete said with a scream,
"Now that I know all there is about steam!"

And as he hung up the phone the boss started to gag,
Because he was left there holding the proverbial bag.

So my phone rang that morning at nine.
"I'd kill you, you bum, if I just had the time!"

"But I don't!" said the boss. "I've a steam job to do,
And no one to do it thanks to you. Thanks to YOU!"

"You're dangerous, Dan," he said, losing control
So this is how Dangerous Dan dug his hole.

I offered to help. Oh yes, there on the job.
"I'll bring my books. You send your mob."

"So what if your men don't know what to do.

With my books and their tools, somehow we'll get through."

And as I hung up the phone I choked back a sob.

For up until then, I'd never been on a job.

But what was there to it? Why, I had this old book!

Hey, I'll just go down there and take a good look.

But when I got to the job I stared, thunderstruck,

For there on the back of this blue pick-up truck,

And straining the tires down into the mud,

And hissing, and bellowing, and crying for blood,

Sat the meanest and heaviest shape known to man.

"What's that?" I asked. "Why, that's the boiler, Dan."

In all of my days I'd never seen such a sight,

And I blinked with my eyes to make sure they saw right.

'Twas a boiler for sure, but I was soon to find,
It was bigger than the one on page ninety-nine.

I'd flipped past that one many times with great ease,
But this beast would soon have me down on my knees.

Yes, we struggled an hour with that son-of-a-gun,
And just when I thought that the battle was won,

The man with the tools asked the kid with the book,
"Where do you want it?" So I took a good look.

And then in my very-most-confident voice,
I said, "Over there is the logical choice."

So we struggled and grunted for ten minutes more,
'Til the beast settled heavily down onto the floor.

And we sat back exhausted. And we all took a break.
As I thought of the decisions I'd soon have to make.

On supplies and returns, and the Hartford Loop, too.

And I opened my book so I'd know what to do.

And I walked to the boiler. And I laid my book down,

When just then my ears heard this crumbling sound.

"Twas the book that had done it. The very last straw!

And that boiler went CRASHING right down through the floor.

Down in the hole the three of us fell,

The boiler, and me, and my textbook as well.

It seems a washing machine, piped into the ground

Had undermined the floor and made it unsound,

And try as I might for the rest of that day,

I could find nothing in my book that would say

What to when a job takes an unfortunate hitch,

So I decided to "pit" that son-of-a-bitch.

"Look here," I said, in a confident voice.

"This, after all, is the logical choice.

"With the waterline difference of an inch or two,

The boiler belongs in a pit. It's true!"

And the men gathered 'round me, and they stared at my book,

And each had his turn to take a good look.

And they all started nodding and they laughed with delight,

For they saw by the book that the hook-up was right!

And once they got over their initial alarm,

They piped in that boiler, and it worked like a charm.

And Dangerous Dan was a hero that day.

And the boss called me up, 'cause he wanted to say

That experience shows, and this really proves it

For he never would have thought of digging that pit.

> Well, I learned me a lesson from my day in the hole,
>
> A lesson that went to the depths of my soul.
>
> There comes a point in your life where you put the books down,
>
> And you learn all the rest from a hole in the ground.

Isn't that fun? The technicians never expected it. I made fun of myself and did something they probably couldn't do, which made me worth a listen.

So use humor in your stories because humor works. But steer clear of the dirty jokes, and *never* tell a story that has racial, sexual, religious, or political content. Do not make fun of *anyone* in your audience. Make fun of yourself. They'll love you for that.

And don't curse. The temptation with a blue-collar audience is there, I know, but resist it. Use your imagination to be more creative with your expressions. *Anyone* can curse; it takes *creativity* to avoid foul language.

I didn't always feel this way. Years ago, I thought that an occasional cussword would endear me to my blue-collar audience. I was wrong, and I learned this lesson in a most expensive way while doing a seminar on heating in Norfolk, Virginia. Norfolk, in case you don't know, is the buckle of the Bible Belt.

I got myself all worked up describing calcium and magnesium deposits that often form on the stem of a valve that is leaking, forming a light-colored crust. "This is commonly known as white s--t," I said.

That line had once gotten me a laugh in New York City, which is why I used it in Norfolk, Virginia. In Norfolk, however, there was only a stony silence that echoes in my memory to this very day. I had over 150 people in the room that day. I was *never* again able to draw a crowd that size in Norfolk.

I learned my lesson.

And if you're showing slides, don't slip in a few slides of scantily clad women as a surprise for the lads. I've had some teachers tell me, "Boy! A couple of babes in bikinis can sure wake up those technicians!" But it's wrong and it will get you into trouble. Don't do it.

And besides, if your audience needs to be woken up, there's something wrong somewhere, right?

Fix it.

Where to find good jokes and stories

Take them from life. That's the best place. Make them real and relevant by putting your own particular twist on them. Play the "What if?" game. You know, "What if it happened *this* way instead of the way it actually happened." Work everyday events over in your mind and turn them into lesson-teaching stories you can use in your lectures.

For instance, I heard a joke a while ago about a guy who was walking on the beach when he found a bottle with a cork in it. He picks it up and opens it and out pops (you guessed it!) a genie. The genie's so happy to be out that he tells the guy he'll grant him one wish.

The guy doesn't even hesitate. He tells the genie that's he's always wanted to go to Hawaii, but he's afraid to fly and he would never go on a ship because ships sometimes sink. He tells the genie to build a road from Los Angeles to Hawaii so that he can drive there (that's *not* the third way).

"Can't do it!" the genie says. "The ocean's much too deep. I'd never be able to drive pilings that far down. Besides, do you have any idea how much concrete and steel that would take? No, it's out of the question. Wish for something else."

The guy thinks for a minute and then says, "Okay, here's my wish. I wish you would explain to me what makes women tick. What makes them laugh? What makes them cry? Why do they act the way they do? Tell me those things and we'll be even."

The genie looks at the guy and says, "How many lanes do you want on that highway?"

That's the way I heard it the first time around. Not long afterwards, my buddy, Mark Eatherton, posted the same joke on my Internet website, but he changed it a bit. In Mark's version, instead of asking the genie to explain what makes women tick, the guy asks the genie to explain the workings of hydronic radiant heating systems. How far apart should the tubes be? How deep should he bury them in the concrete? What's the right water temperature? What's the best way to control the system?

To which the genie replies, "How many lanes do you want on that highway?"

It works even better, doesn't it? And you don't make the women angry when you tell it Mark's way either!

So do it.

139

Go to the library or to your local bookstore and look in the Humor section. Use the Internet. There are a million jokes at your fingertips. Go through them. Find things that are relevant to your topic. And remember, a Polish, Irish, Jewish or *whatever* joke can easily become a technician- or teacher joke if you work it around a bit. You'll also find resource books written specifically for public speakers. These are filled with jokes and anecdotes (tiny tales) that you can work into your lecture to make it more interesting.

Look to your friends and relatives for jokes and anecdotes. Some of *my* relatives are the biggest jokes I know!

If you can, work in some humor that's relevant or topical to the area you're working in. For instance, I was hired to do a lecture in Maine. I drove there from my home on Long Island. When I crossed over into Maine from New Hampshire I spotted a sign for a rest area. I decided to stop to use the facilities. When I was walking back to my car I noticed that there was a sign over the trashcans that read, "It is not healthy to rummage through the trashcans!" That cracked me up.

The next day, as I was starting my seminar, I mentioned that Maine was the only state that I have ever traveled to where they have to tell you not to dig in the garbage. "Gosh," I said, "that seems like something your mother should have taught you a long time ago, eh? What the heck's going on up here?"

It got a good laugh, and then one of the guys in the back row shouted, "That sign's there for you *tourists*!"

This got an even bigger laugh – at my expense.

And that made it even better!

Join Toastmasters International. You'll not only get to practice your public speaking, you'll also meet other people who are interested in teaching, and who have *loads* of stories and jokes to share with you.

Watch and listen to great storytellers like Garrison Keillor. His tales of the citizens of Lake Woebegone are brilliant examples of how to tell a story.

Read *anything* by Mark Twain or Charles Dickens.

Listen to audio books while driving.

Fill your life with wonderful books and read all the time.

Aloha also means good-bye, you know

We were on the plane flying back to New York City. My sweet wife, The Lovely Marianne, tanned and rested in her coach seat, turned to me and said, "If you don't tell me the third way to get to Hawaii, I'm going to consult a divorce lawyer as soon as we land."

"Yikes!" I said. "Have I upset my little wahine?"

"Spill the beans!" she demanded, shaking her little fist at me.

"Okay," I said. "You're sure you're ready?"

"I'm *ready*!" she hissed.

"Then just turn the question around and ask it another way."

"What do you mean?"

"I mean, instead of asking, 'How can I get *to* Hawaii?' try asking it this way. I'm already *in* Hawaii. How could I possibly have gotten here?"

"I could have been *born* here!" she shouted.

"Bingo," I said.

"You hung me up for a week over that," she said.

"Nope, you hung *yourself* up."

"Why was that so hard to do?" she asked.

"Because sometimes you have to turn the question around a bit to find the answer. That's what technicians do when they're stumped on a trouble call, you know. At least that's what the good ones do. They ask the question in a different way – and the answer jumps right up at them!"

"I *still* may call that divorce lawyer," my sweet bride said.

"Why?"

"Maybe he can turn *you* around," she said.

But she didn't.

See how you can turn a good story into a lesson?

And I've probably held your attention through this whole chapter by using this running joke, haven't I? I've strung a bunch of stories together using the thread of the Hawaii story to keep your interest. You wanted to get to the punch line, didn't you? I held it back on purpose. That's obvious. But think about *why* I did that.

Imagine you were in my class and I kept teasing you with the punch line. I'd get to a point during the day where

I'd say, "Do you have any questions?" You'd say, "Yeah! What's the third way to get to Hawaii?" I'd smile at you and answer, "That's an *excellent* question!" and then move on with my lecture.

I'd do this to you *all day long* – and you'd pay attention all day long. And you'd get the connection between the three ways to get to Hawaii and being a good troubleshooter.

Right?

And we'd have *fun*.

It's sort of like that strange gauge with the "Atmospheres" and "Minutes" scales I was telling you about before.

Remember?

Hmm?

CHAPTER SIX
The power of fun

The difference between work and play

This retired guy had a house near an elementary school. Across the front of his house he had a white picket fence. Every day a half-dozen young boys walked past his house on their way home from school. They each had a stick that they would drag across the pickets, making a racket and messing up the paint job. The old-timer knew that the kids were just having fun and that if he ordered them to knock it off, they'd just want to have even *more* fun with his fence.

So he came up with a plan. One day he met the boys as they were approaching the fence. They all hid their sticks behind their backs.

"Hello!" the old-timer said. "I was wondering if I could ask you boys a favor. Every day, you walk by my house with those sticks and you tap on my fence."

The boys tried even harder to hide their sticks, figuring the old-timer was about to lower the boom.

"Well," he continued, "I have to tell you, I just *love* the sound that those sticks make when they ratchet across my fence. It sort of reminds me of a stage full of tap dancers! You know what I mean?" He mimicked a tap dancer, albeit a very *slow* tap dancer. "Boys," he said, "I'm wondering if you wouldn't mind going by my house *twice* a day instead of once." The boys looked at him as if he was crazy. "Yes, I'm wondering if you'd be willing to double-back and do it again every day. Like this." He snatched the stick from the boy closest to him and tapped his way down the fence and back. "Oh, I *love* that!" he exclaimed. "But I'm not asking you to do it for free," he quickly explained. "I'll pay you each a dollar a day! It's worth that much to me."

Well, the boys jumped at this, of course. Imagine getting paid for having fun! They accepted his offer and rattled his fence twice a day for the next four days. He was there to pay them every time.

On the fifth day, however, he met them with a sad expression. "Boys," he said. "I'm sorry to tell you that there's been a drop in the stock market, and that this has affected my pension. I won't be able to pay you a dollar a day anymore, but I *can* still pay you each fifty cents a day, and I'm hoping you'll be able to see your way clear to still do the job at that lower rate of pay. Can you? *Please*?"

The boys weren't happy with this development, but they reluctantly accepted and for the next two days gave his fence a half-hearted, fifty-cent going over. One of the boys suggested that they stop going to the old-timer's house, but another said, "No! It's our job. We *have to* do it!"

The following day, the old-timer met the boys at the end of the fence, and this time he looked even sadder. "I don't know quite how to break this to you fellas, but there's been *another* downturn in the market and I'll only be able to pay you *twenty-five cents apiece* from now on."

The boys looked at each other and without even a consultation they said, "*Forget* it! We won't be back anymore. You think you can *cheat* us, but you're wrong, old man!" They stormed off in a huff.

And the old man strolled back into his house with a very satisfied grin on his face.

Fun makes the time fly!

For those kids, what began as fun became a job. And after it became a job, it stopped being as much fun. The money became the important thing. Before long, they even forgot how to *have* fun!

A lot of technicians go through a similar process. When they first escape from school and get out in the real world they can hardly believe that someone would be willing to pay them for tinkering with machines. Hey, they'd be willing to do that for free!

But as time goes by, and as money issues crop up (and union issues, and family issues, and office-politics issues), the fun often goes out of the job and the job turns into drudgery. People can't wait for the day to end. They can't wait for their vacation. They can't wait for their retirement. There's even a restaurant called Thank God It's Friday, for Pete's sake! They'd quit that stinking job in a minute if they could only hit the lottery.

And then someone tells them that they have to leave the relative freedom of their trucks to spend a day listening to the likes of *you*. In a *classroom*? Ugh!

But imagine how they're going to feel when you make that class *fun*.

And you *will* make it fun, won't you? There's no reason why you *shouldn't*, and if you make it fun for them, it will also be fun for *you*. And what could be better than that?

Always remember that these guys are used to moving around. They're not used to sitting still. You have to "pay" them to make them sit still for that long.

So you'll "pay" them with fun.

Besides, people don't realize how much they're learning when they're having fun. I can't tell you how many times a technician has come up to me after a seminar and said something like, "You know, Dan, at first I thought that you were some sort of comedian. I mean you're up there joking around with us and telling all these stories. I started out thinking that I was wasting my time by being here. But then, around lunchtime, I started to realize that I had picked up an *enormous* amount of useful information in a couple of hours. I can't even remember exactly when it all came to me. I was having too much fun! You just sort of slipped it in, didn't you?"

Yeah, I did.

Fun makes learning painless.

Delicious medicine

In 1973, Marianne and I got a used cocker spaniel from the Dog Pound. We named him Rusty. Rusty was a good dog but he often got sick. I'd take him to the vet and the vet would guy charge me a bunch and then give me some pills. These I had to give to Rusty three times a day.

Rusty would lie in front of the refrigerator and moan and sneeze. I'd get out the pills and try my best to get that old dog to take one. I'd hold it in my hand and he'd just look at me with those sad eyes and roll over. I'd push the pill toward his mouth and he'd growl at me. I'd pry his mouth open, stick the pill down his throat, and massage his neck while holding his jaws clamped shut, all the while trying to keep my fingers attached to my hand. As soon as I let go of his mouth, Rusty would spit the pill on the floor, get up, and hobble away.

I didn't know what to do, so I called the vet. "He won't take his medicine," I said. "What should I do?"

"Put the pill in a lump of cream cheese," the vet said. "He'll eat the pill because he won't be able to taste it. He'll be so busy gobbling up the good stuff that the pill will just sneak by without him even noticing that he's getting it."

The vet was right. From that day on, Rusty came running whenever he heard me shaking that pill bottle.

So learn a lesson from an old dog. Wrap all your lectures in something delicious.

Fun with props

If you ever find yourself having to teach a group of New Hampshire technicians about radiant heat, try putting a brick on a hotplate. Heat the brick it until it's hotter than the center of the Earth. Then place said brick on a glass plate and watch the whole works explode.

Been there. Done that. Got the scars to prove it.

The brick and the plate are called props. The explosion is called a *total* surprise. The first part is fun; the second part is dumb – but *also* fun if the joke is on you.

Props can make your lecture, um . . . *interesting*.

I once went to a magic shop with my daughters to get some stuff for Halloween. I was browsing around the place when I spotted a prop book that looked pretty neat. It was hollowed out and it had a wick inside of it that you were supposed to drench with lighter fluid. There was an electronic igniter connected to a battery and a small button that was hidden near the bottom of the book's spine. When I pressed the small button, the igniter sparked and the lighter fluid burst into flames. When I heard the Whoosh! I knew it was time to open the book. If I did it properly I'd wind up holding a foot-high flame in my hands. Pretty neat, eh? A flaming book. Wow!

Anyway, I used this thing for a few months and I thought I was pretty hot stuff. I was the Great Danzo! I'd say to the technicians, "Gentlemen, here we have a book on the subject of *combustion*." I'd open the cover, release the inferno, and amaze and amuse the crowd every time. I was quickly becoming a legend among technicians. I'd hold their attention all day long with my pyrotechnics. Wow, a burning book! A book about *combustion*. Get it? Combustion? Burning?

Wow.

The last time I did the trick, however, I somehow forgot that I had spilled lighter fluid all over my hands. When I opened the cover, a *lot* more than the book burst into flames that day.

Wow!

YEOW!

You had to be there.

They still talk about it.

Props. They're not just a job; they're an adventure!

I've seen fire and I've seen . . . rain

When I'm talking about centrifugal pumps I have a little trick that always keeps the technicians on their toes. I'll fill a bucket with water and start swinging it over my head. The technicians in the front rows *especially* enjoy this. When I get it going in a break-the-handle fury, I shout out, "What's holding the water in the bucket?" They shout back, "Centrifugal force!" I yell, "No *way*! It's the bottom of the *bucket* that's holding the water in the bucket!"

That's always good for a belly laugh.

"Now," I continue, "do you know Sir Isaac Newton?" Blank stares. "He invented that cookie?" (laughs) "And he also gave us The First Law of Inertia! A body in motion (big swing of the water bucket) tends to stay in motion (bigger swing) until it is interfered with by something else (huge swing!). Now when I let go of this bucket (Whoa!) . . . it will fly out in a straight line, due . . . to . . . centrifugal . . . force. The water, of course . . . will remain *inside* the bucket because of Newtonian physics (biggest swing of all. I mean, the thing is practically pulling me off my feet at this point). And one . . . of . . . you . . . lucky . . . people . . . will . . . come . . . to . . . fully . . . understand . . . Newton's . . . First . . . Law (people start ducking under tables, running for the exits) as . . . you . . . catch . . . this . . . bucket . . . *and* . . . the . . . water . . .in . . . your . . . outstretched . . . arms . . . like . . . an . . . NFL . . . wide . . . receiver. Are . . . you . . . ready? WHO'S IT GONNA BE?"

Believe it or not, I once actually had a guy take me up on this. To our collective astonishment, it actually worked! The water and the bucket traveled at the same rate of velocity and he caught the whole works without spilling a drop. Newton was right!

It didn't work as well the *second* time we tried it, however.

On *most* days, I'll just suddenly stop swinging the bucket. I'll smile and say, "But I'm not going to let it go today, folks. You see, I've learned that when I hit that special someone with this gallon of water, that special someone usually tries to teach *me* about Newton's *Second* Law, which states that for every action . . . there's an equal and opposite *reaction*."

This sort of thing works with technicians. They sit on the edge of their chairs and laugh like mad because this sort of thing is *fun*.

There was a day I shall not forget when I managed to hit the chandelier on my first big swing. This young guy in the middle of the front row got the worst of it. About two quarts of water hit him square in the puss. The other half-gallon somehow managed to go *under* the table and right up between his legs. It was pretty impressive, and he will *never* take centrifugal force for granted. Of that I can assure you.

It could have been worse, though. He could have been on *fire*.

You can find laws of physics in *most* everyday items. Spend some spare time looking at the books written for kids who want to enter Science Fairs at their schools. These books are filled with simple experiments that *beautifully* illustrate basic principles technicians need to know. The Mister Wizard books are my personal favorites.

Get a metal, half-gallon can – the sort that painters use to hold turpentine. You can pick one up in most paint stores. Pour about a half-inch of water into the can and put the can on a stove or a hotplate (and *please* make sure there's no turpentine left in the can).

Boil the water and screw the cap on the top of the can while the water's still boiling. Make sure it's tight. Now, take the can off the heat and watch what happens when the trapped steam in the can condenses. The steam caves in, leaving a partial vacuum in its place. All of a sudden, it looks like some invisible giant reaches in and *crushes* the can. I mean, the thing just *implodes* right before your eyes! What an impression this makes! It's a basic law of physics brought to life.

And then there's this one.

Get an empty plastic milk container (the gallon size works best for this). Fill it with water and turn it upside down so that the water can drop safely into a bucket. Explain to the technicians that there is, in physics, something called Boyle's Law. Gases will expand to fill the space allowed them. And when gases expand, the pressure of the gas drops. Right around then the sides of the milk container will begin to collapse as the greater atmospheric pressure on the outside of the container exerts itself on the lowering pressure inside the container.

Seeing is believing, right?

Get a bottle of soda (or soda pop, pop, coke, whatever!) and shake it up real well with the cap on. Explain to the technicians that, in physics, there is something called Henry's Law. Gases will dissolve in liquids in proportion to the pressure and temperature applied to the liquid. As you shake the soda, some of the carbon dioxide in the soda escapes and moves to the top where it exerts a pressure on the liquid. There's a *lot* of gas trapped in that liquid. When you release the pressure by popping the top (and make sure you do this while standing *very* close to the technician of your choice), the gases, now under a lesser pressure, will escape from the liquid! *Bam*! Another law of physics brought to life.

And the best part is no one's on fire!

Props are good. Use them whenever you can. The technicians will remember you for years – assuming they survive the experience.

Fun with stories

Make your stories as personal as they can be. And by all means, feel free to borrow a good story and make it your own. There's nothing illegal, immoral, or fattening about this. Your goal is to *teach*. The stories will help you do that. It's okay to borrow and to use your imagination to make your stories more fun.

A wise man once said that if you steal from one person it is called plagiarism, but if you steal from everyone it is called research.

I highly recommend research.

I once had a guy come to a seminar and tell me a story that was hilarious. It also taught a great technical lesson. I immediately adopted the story as my own and told it the following week in another state. It got peals of laughter and it helped me get my message across to the technicians. The next day I told the story again in yet another state to even *more* laughter. I kept working that story, and I kept getting bigger and bigger laughs. And since I have a *mighty* fine imagination, I started to add colors and flavors, and even odors to it. After a couple of years, the story was even growing fur, and I was starting to believe that it had actually happened as told.

But actually it had not.

That didn't stop *this* boy, though! Oh no! I worked that story into a frenzy! One day I was telling it back in the original city where I had first heard it. I didn't remember that this was THE city where I had first heard THE story because cities start to blend together like smoke when you spend as much time on the road as I did. I was just up there, telling THE story.

I got about halfway into it and the crowd loved it. And that's when I spotted the guy who had first told *me* the story. He was sitting right there in the middle of the room, and he was giving me a *most* curious look.

I was busted, but there was no way out. I had already pushed THE story over the edge and I was just hanging onto it at that point. I had to see it through to its hilarious climax.

And all the while, he was giving me this *really* strange look.

At the first break, the guy came running up to the front of the room. Here we go, I thought. I'm sunk. "Dan," he said. "I was at your seminar a couple of years ago. I don't know if you remember."

"Well, your face *does* look familiar. Welcome back!" I sputtered.

"You know that story you told before?" he said, not to be denied his moment of anecdote reclamation.

"Uh, yes," I said sheepishly.

"Well, you're not gonna *believe* this, but a similar thing happened to *me* once!"

And then he told me the original story all over again – as if for the very first time.

And it was then that I realized that my crazy imagination had so twisted his story that it had become something entirely new – something that really *was* mine alone. Something that helped me to teach technicians.

And that's what really mattered. Teachers *teach*.

And that's why it never bothers me when somebody uses any of my stories. I acknowledge that they're just doing research.

So have *fun* with your stories. Make them outrageous. I've told crowds of technicians that The Lovely Marianne and I raised our children to be experts at steam and hot water heating. When they were small we read to them not from the nursery rhyme books, but from the engineering tomes that are the bibles of my industry! When the girls were small, we took them to the amusement park and my little cherubs *insisted* on looking at the motors on the Ferris wheel and the roller coaster. They wanted to know the horsepower, amperage draw, and phase of those motors – even though my little darlings were only *this* tall (pretty short, eh?).

When the technicians doubted this, I put the family-album photos up on the screen. I had prepared this very special album for those of little faith. Here we have my daughter Colleen, fast asleep in her bed and snuggling not a Teddy Bear, but a Stilson wrench. Next we have her twin sister, Erin. As you can see, Erin is opening the box containing the centrifugal pump we bought her for her birthday. Doesn't she look happy? Notice how the candles on the cake glow so softly. Look at that excitement in her eyes! And here's Colleen on that very same day with her new clock thermostat. And what's this? Ah, the four little cherubs gathered around the Christmas tree in their pajamas. They *loved* the heating products Santa left for them. Look! It's an outdoor-air reset control with proportional-integral-derivative logic!

That brought down the house. The technicians sat up and listened for the rest of the day. You know why? Because they *never* knew what I was going to do next, and because they were having so much *fun*.

Fun killers

Unless it's required by law, by licensing, or by the folks who are paying you, *don't* give tests.

Tests kill fun.

Tests create anxiety and put people on edge.

If you're a good teacher, you won't need a test to prove to yourself that you've been effective. You'll *see* it in their eyes. You'll *hear* it in their comments after the session. And you'll *witness* it in their work in the days to come.

Instead of tests, go for feedback, and go for it all day long. Ask them questions. Throw brainteasers their way to see if they're paying attention. Ask them to repeat something you told them earlier ("Who remembers how many BTUs there are in a square foot of radiation?). Praise the person who gets it right. Give 'em a lollipop!

Lollipops beat tests every day of the week.

It's fun to participate!

You ever hear of habeas corpus? It's on TV all the time. You know, on the lawyer shows. It's a legal term that means, "You should have the body." Lawyers use it when they want to get someone to show up in court.

Some technicians subscribe to the School of Habeas Corpus. They show up in the morning and declare, "You wanted my body? Well, here it is. My mind, however, is elsewhere."

It's your job to get these people to participate in your seminar. You'll have to convince them that participation is *fun*! I once had a technician look me right in the eye and say, "I'm only here because my boss *made* me come." I smiled and said, "Well that's *great*, because we're gonna have fun. I really don't care if you learn anything today. I just want to make sure you have *fun*, pal. The heck with your boss."

That screwed him up a bit. He didn't know what to say.

Then I taught him a lot of stuff.

You want to get people to participate? Present them with a situation where there's something in it for *them*. I once started a seminar by asking everyone in the room to raise their right hand. I made sure I said please. "*Please* raise your right hand," I said, and they did. I think they thought I was going to swear them in or something.

Once they all had their right hands up I just smiled and said, "Thanks! I just wanted to see if you'd do it."

They all put their hands down and stared at me. Some of them giggled a bit.

"Would you *please* raise your *left* hand," I said.

Only about half the people in the room did it this time. More people giggled. "Hey, I said *please*, didn't I? Aren't we friends anymore?" I stood up there in the front of the room, smiling like the village idiot and pumping my left hand in the air. I waved at them with my left land. I said, "*Pleeeeesssseeee?*" More of them raised their left hands. "Thank you *so* much!" I said. "Now, will you *please* stand up, lift your chair over your head and look under it?"

No one did it.

"Please?"

Nothing.

"Did I mention that I taped a hundred bucks under one of the chairs early this morning?" I said. "If it's under *your* chair, you can have it. All you have to do is get up, pick up the chair, look under it, and if the hundred is there, it's yours."

At this point, someone usually gets up and looks under his chair. Others start to laugh and then get up themselves. The more they laugh, the faster people get up. They do this because laughter has introduced *fun* into the seminar, and it's okay to do something silly as long as you're laughing – and as long as everyone else is *also* doing it.

Now, while they're searching under their chairs, I lift a chair I've set next to my table and find the hundred. "Wow!" I say. "Look at *this*! I am sooo lucky!"

The place goes nuts.

"I won yesterday, *too*!" I say.

They go even more nuts.

This is a neat way to start a seminar because not only did I get them to participate right up front, I also tricked them and that makes them feel like I'm worth listening to. Remember we talked about this earlier? I also got to make the point that most people (customers included) won't do what you want them to do *unless there's something in it for them*. That's a powerful lesson for technicians because it helps get them focused on paying attention to the *customer's* needs and not just their own.

It's also a powerful lesson for you.

You want those technicians to listen to you?

Think about what's in it for *them*.

Now, here's another thing I want you to consider. When you ask the group a question, do **not** answer it yourself! You've seen teachers do this, haven't you? "Does anyone know how many feet there are in a mile?" And then before you can open your mouth, the guy says, "There are five-thousand-two-hundred-eighty feet in a mile."

And he does that all day long.

So the technicians say to themselves, Great! This is going to be an easy day. This bozo's going to answer all of his questions *for* me. No reason for me to break out the ol' brain today! Nope, all I have to do is deliver my body. It's here, so good night!

Let me say it again. *Do not under any circumstances answer your own questions.* You will play right into that School of Habeas Corpus thing. You will be speaking to bodies, but not minds. Be prepared to stand in front of that room and wait *forever* if necessary for an answer from that group. You *can* out wait them. Trust me on this. The silence will make them nervous *long* before it makes you nervous. Remember that *you're* in charge in that room. Try it like this:

"Does anyone know how many days there are in a week?"

Silence.

Blank stares.

More silence.

"Hello? It's *your* turn."

Silence.

You just stand there smiling at them.

You start to whistle the tune from *Jeopardy*. They start to chuckle.

"If it was just you and me having lunch," you say, "and if I asked you how many days there are in the week, would you just look at me like that? Would you give me that blank stare? Nah, I'd bet you'd *answer* me, wouldn't you? Now, as I was saying, does anyone know how many days there are in a week?"

Finally, someone says, "Seven."

You throw up your arms and shout, "OH, THANK YOU! YOU *SPOKE* TO ME! I FEEL POSITIVELY FULFILLED!"

After that, you'll be okay. You tell them, "It's a *conversation*. Just you and me. That's all that matters today. We're going to talk to each other today and we're going to have fun. You'll see. *Okay*?"

Silence.

More silence.

Somebody finally says, "Okay!"

And now you *are* okay.

Okay?

One final thought on participation. *Never* give the technicians anything to read while you're talking to them. They'll look at the printed material whenever you try to make eye contact with them to get an answer to your question. The more you try to get them to participate, the more they'll read what you gave them. It could be the back of a ketchup bottle. It doesn't matter. If you give it to them, they'll read it – just to avoid your eyes.

The same goes for PowerPoint. Your slides should have photos and diagrams, never *ever* words.

Never!

Okay?

OKAY?

CHAPTER SEVEN
Tool time

I know you can't see this but . . .

I once went to a lecture where the teacher turned his back on me, squinted at the screen and said, "I know you can't see this but . . ." And then he added something like, "Well anyway, the wire goes from terminal A to terminals C and D. It's *really* hard to see, I know. I can barely see it myself from here. I didn't have much time to put this program together. Anyway, the catalog shows it *much* better, but they're too expensive to hand out these days, so please just bear with me for the next half-hour while I bore you to tears with my indecipherable slides that look like linguine with clam sauce. Okay?"

Here's a good question. If that knucklehead *knows* that I can't see that slide, why the heck is he showing it to me?

I won't keep you in suspense. He's showing it to me because he doesn't understand how to use the tools of his trade. Which these days are mainly hands-on stuff and PowerPoint slides.

Here's what you ought to know.

Back in the day

When I started teaching, I used a lot of 35-mm slide projections. The bad news with those was that I had to shut off the lights in the room, and that, of course, invited sleep. I had to work extra hard in the dark to keep their attention.

Beyond the darkness, the other challenge with slides was that I was tempted to turn my back on my audience to see and describe what they were looking at. But on the other hand, since we were all in the dark they probably didn't even realize that I had turned my back

And that wasn't good.

I memorized what I was going to say about each slide, of course. Those slides were linear, like PowerPoint. If someone asked me a question that didn't have to do with that slide or the one on deck, I had to go off on a tangent, and that was always awkward. It turned into a conversation between me and that one tech, and that left the other techs on their own for a bit. In the dark.

Slides, since they showed pictures and not words, were a good way to prepare for PowerPoint.

More on that in a minute.

Video?

You have two ways to go here. You can use a TV monitor with a DVD, or you can use a video projector with a DVD. You can also live-steam from the Internet. What you do will depend a lot on your budget and the size of the group you're teaching.

TV monitors give you sharp pictures, but you have to make sure the screen is large enough for all to see. Pay especial attention to where you place the monitor. It should be high enough so that people's heads don't block other people's views. The monitor should also be far enough back so that those on the sides of the room can see the screen. I once lectured to a group of 300 people and used TV monitors, but there were four monitors positioned throughout the room, each taking its feed from a single VCR. The hotel that the sponsor used was particularly good at setting up A/V equipment, so everything worked out well.

Today's video projectors are small and relatively inexpensive. A video-projected image will be wider than it is high. This is standard TV formatting and there are screens made specifically for video projectors that will accommodate an image of this shape. Video screens are also coated with a special material to enhance the brightness of the projected image. They're not absolutely necessary, but they *are* a plus if they're available.

I traveled with my own projector. I often spoke in conference rooms that were tight because there were so many techs at the meetings. My projector was the type that could be very close to the screen (like four feet away) and still fill a six-foot screen with a great image. Look for one of those if you're going to be working in tight quarters.

And please give a *lot* of thought to what you're going to show the technicians before you consider video. Ask yourself if it wouldn't be more effective to let them watch the video on their own online. In other words, do they *really* need you to babysit them while they watch a movie? Remember that the focus should be on *you* as the thread that holds all of this together. The video is a *tool* that you're using – nothing more. If it can stand by itself, maybe it should stand by itself. If it's a video that a manufacturer has put together to demonstrate their product, perhaps the technicians should watch it on their own. Does it really belong within your seminar? *That's* the question.

Maybe it does, maybe it doesn't.

Please don't use it just to fill time.

I'd like you to carefully consider these questions before you show a video in a group setting.

In my work with heating technicians, I've used what I call "Basement Movies." These are short (10-15 minute) videos that I've shot inside buildings. In most cases, I just walked through a building, showing the pipes, valves, boilers, and controls, while talking. I'm not in the shot. I'd usually have someone who was working on the job in the shot. I'd talk to him from off camera, just as if we were in the boiler room together. He'd respond by pointing at system components and commenting on them. It's a simple point-of-view technique and it makes the audience feel as if they're right there on the job with you. These videos were amateurish, certainly, but they were *very* effective with technicians because they were so *real*. In most cases, I started with an exterior shot of the building and then moved inside. I'd explain along the way where I was and where we were going next. For instance:

[EXTERIOR SHOT OF THE BUILDING] "Here we are at 125 Desolation Boulevard. As you can see, it's a five-story building, built sometime during the 1920s. Let's go down to the basement and take a look in the boiler room."

[CUT TO BASEMENT SHOT] "We're in the boiler room now."

[CAMERA PANS AROUND THE ROOM] "As you can see, the equipment is pretty old and run down. Boy, look at the age of this stuff!"

[CAMERA STOPS PANNING WHEN IT REACHES FREDDY] "Hey, Freddy! How you doing? "

[FREDDY WAVES AND SAYS HELLO] Freddy's the superintendent of the building. Why don't you tell us a bit about what's going on here."

From there, Freddy would just start chatting with me. There was literally no rehearsal with any of the Basement Movies, and only one "take." Usually, we'd be making the movie after we'd figured out what was causing the trouble, so it was really a reenactment of what we'd done that day. It all came across as *very* natural. If Freddy were to indicate that the trouble started in one of the apartments upstairs, I might say something like, "Let's take a look up in that apartment right now, Freddy." Then I'd shut off the camera and we'd go upstairs. Once there, I'd start the camera again, pan around the room and say, "Well, here we are in the apartment you were telling us about. Is this the radiator that was giving you trouble, Freddy?"

And we'd take it from there.

What you're looking for if you make a Basement Movie is continuity. Remember that the technicians will be watching the Basement Movie months and perhaps *years* from now. They've never been in that building. They're depending on you to tell them where they are in relation to where they just were. Pay close attention to continuity the next time you're watching a TV show or a movie. Without continuity the only one who will understand what's going on in that video is you – and maybe Freddy.

Once the Basement Movie was over, the technicians and I would discuss it. It was also very easy to pause these tapes along the way and point out key elements of the job – things that may be causing the trouble. I could also stop the tape at any point and back it up to make a point a second time. I'd often stop the tape and switch over to an overhead projector to show a cutaway drawing of an item that appeared on the video. This gave the technicians a better idea of what we had to deal with on that particular job. It was all very real. It made everyone feel as if we were on an actual job.

Can you feel the difference between the interactive nature of the Basement Movies and just sitting there watching the technicians as they watch a manufacturer's video about a product? The first is active; the second is passive. Active is *so* much better in a classroom setting.

The "Basement Movies" cost literally nothing to make and I found them to be as effective as the corporate stuff equipment manufacturers produce for tens of thousands of dollars. Don't get me wrong, those videos are great for a one-on-one showing, but the Basement Movies just worked better in a seminar setting with technicians.

There's one other thing to consider with video. You must be prepared for the equipment to break down, and you must always have back-ups of your videos. Store them in the Cloud and you'll always have access to them.

Flip charts

Flip charts are inexpensive and fine for small groups. Make sure everyone can see what you're drawing and make sure that you can draw. Use broad-tipped markers with dark ink for the best visibility. If you're going to write words, make sure you know how to spell them. Sounds silly, I know, but why risk embarismint, eh . . . I mean *embarrassment*?

If you think you might misspell certain key words during your presentation, trace them lightly on top of the flip chart's pages beforehand. The technicians won't be able to see what you've traced, and it will give you an edge when it comes to the spelling. This is also a neat way to leave notes for yourself so that you don't miss any important points. You can also trace any diagrams you'll be doing during your presentation. Then all you'll have to do is go over the diagram with the dark marker when you get to the appropriate time.

One of the nice things about a flip chart is that you can tear off each page as you finish it and then tape the page to the walls of the meeting room as a reminder of where you've been. The technicians can refer back to these as the day goes by.

If a technician has a question, he can also come up to the front of the room and make a sketch on the flip chart. This will give him a way to express himself visually and it can lead to a better understanding between you and the group. But take care that you don't get into a one-on-one conversation with a technician who steps up to make a sketch. You're liable to lose everyone else in the process.

A drawback of the flip chart, of course, is that you have to turn your back on the group while you're drawing, but if you plan properly, you can limit the time you spend doing this.

You'll also need an easel to hold the flip chart. Get one with a tray to hold your markers and make sure that the easel is secure when you set it up. Tighten all the screws before you begin so that it doesn't go crashing to the floor the first time you touch it.

Blackboards

Blackboards remind most people of school, and that's the biggest thing they have going against them. They often conjure bad memories and they work only with small groups, and even there not so well. Each time you write on a blackboard, you turn your back on the technicians. That breaks your eye contact and makes it more difficult for you to stay connected.

And chalk is messy. It breaks. It squeaks. You have to clean the board. You have to bang the erasers to get the chalk dust out of them (that was the job for the bad boys, if I recall). Some people are allergic to chalk dust.

I can't stand blackboards.

White boards

This is a more modern version of the blackboard. Instead of chalk you use colored markers. The result looks a bit better. You can wipe the ink with a special eraser, and while it does look cleaner than a blackboard, you have to use a special chemical to clean your white board from time to time (and some people are allergic to chemicals). If you use the wrong type of marker, you'll ruin the white board for all time.

Here again, you have to turn your back on the technicians and that's not good because you break eye contact and you're liable to get hit with a beer can or pizza crust if your lecture is lousy.

Some companies try to save a few bucks by using the white board as both a place to write *and* project. This is a major mistake. Projection screens have a special coating to diffuse the bright light of a projector. White boards are as smooth as glass. They bounce that projector glare right back into the eyes of the audience. It's very annoying, no matter where you're sitting in the room. It's like looking into high-beams. Spend the money on a proper screen to cover the white board if you're going to need both for your presentation.

System mock-ups

If it lends itself to your subject, consider building a mock-up of the system that you'll be describing. Make it in such a way that you'll be able to assemble it during your lecture. This has tremendous appeal to technicians because it's so real – and it's *there*.

I once gave a series of lectures on residential, hot-water heating. I wanted a way to show what went where in the boiler room, and I wanted to use the actual system components if I could. The challenge was that I had to transport this thing to hotels all over the place and a boiler alone weighs about 400 pounds. I realized that, for my purposes, the piping and the components were more important than the boiler itself, so I built a box out of plywood and used it to support the system components in much the same way that a boiler would on an actual job. The box was about four feet high and two feet wide. I put it on wheels and built compartments inside so I could stow all the components I'd be screwing onto the box.

When I did that seminar I just wheeled the box into the hotel, opened the hinged door and took out all the parts. Then, as I gave my talk, I'd put the system together. I'd point at the box and say, "This is a boiler. It's a *wood* boiler." That was usually good for a laugh because there *are* "wood" boilers. They *burn* wood, though; they're not *made* of wood. During the breaks, the technicians would come up to the front and fiddle with my make-believe boiler room. They'd stand around it and touch it. I always got a big kick out of that. They just *loved* to touch it. There's nothing quite like hands-on when it comes to teaching technicians.

I had a similar experience years ago when I worked for the manufacturers' rep. We sold big centrifugal pumps, the sort used to move the water that heats and cools high-rise buildings. We worked in New York City, which is home to many large consulting engineering firms. These mechanical engineers wrote the specifications for much of the work that was going on across the country. My old boss decided that it would be a good idea for me to put together a canned speech on centrifugal pumps that I could give to those engineers. The speech lasted about 45 minutes, which was perfect because I was going to give it in the engineers' offices during lunchtime. We paid for the sandwiches in exchange for their attention. It's the sort of arrangement that goes on daily between consulting engineers and manufacturers' reps in big cities.

An associate who knew the engineers very well would make the appointments, and she and I would travel by foot or by taxi around Manhattan. We did one lecture every day, five days a week. We saw more than 60 engineering firms.

Since I wouldn't have access to a projector during these lunchtime meetings I had a graphics artist make up a series of technical diagrams for me. I had each diagram enlarged to 24" X 18" and mounted on a stiff piece of cardboard. This was a good size to use with a group of about 15 people seated around a conference table. I packed the diagrams in an artist's portfolio case and I brought along a small easel, the sort you'd use to hold up a page of notes while typing. I wrote *my* notes on the backs of each diagram. When I held up the diagram for all to see, I was staring right at my notes! When I put the diagram on the easel, the notes remained right in front of me. It worked out very well, and it gave the impression that I was speaking off the cuff. I wasn't! In fact, I was very nervous because these were some of the sharpest people in the industry. These were New York City mechanical engineers, and I have never taken an engineering course in my life. All of my knowledge came from reading books and being in basements.

But you know what? That's what I had going for me. I spent more time in boiler rooms than they did. Most of these engineers were tied to their desks. And that's why I decided to also bring a display with me on this tour. I needed something *real*. I had one of the technicians in our office make a cutaway of an actual centrifugal pump. We left the motor back at the office to save weight and just traveled with the business end of the thing. It weighed about 75 pounds and I used a heavy-duty luggage carrier to drag it around the streets of Manhattan. I got in pretty good shape lifting it in and out of the trunks of taxicabs.

We'd get to some engineering firm's conference room and I'd manhandle the pump up onto the table – right next to my little easel. As I lectured, I'd point to each part, turn the shaft, put my finger in the impeller and generally fuss over the pump. At the end of the lecture there were questions, of course, but then the wildest thing happened (and it happened *every* day).

The engineers would come up to the cutaway and point to each part, turn the shaft, put their fingers in the impeller and generally fuss over the pump.

They couldn't keep their hands off the thing!

As I had suspected, most had never seen one in real life. They specified thousands of them, but they had never actually *seen* one, let alone touch the insides of one. To most of these engineers, a centrifugal pump was a blue circle with an arrow on a building plan. It was like watching bunches of little kids playing with a new toy.

We made some great headway with that tour because what I had to show them was so *real*.

The next time you're at a trade show, notice the booths that are getting the most attention. My guess is that they will be the companies that are using hands-on displays with moving parts.

Taco Comfort Solutions, a major manufacturer of hot-water-heating components, makes a small circulator for house heating. At the trade shows, they had what they called a Fast-Hands competition. They challenged the techs to open the circulator with a screwdriver, change the internal parts, and put the thing back together. The fastest hands won a prize and techs lined up for this. They all came away with the sense that Taco circulators are easily repaired. They had fun learning that. It was brilliant.

Technicians just can't resist those displays. Neither can engineers.

Keep it in mind.

PowerPoint

In 1998, I took my daughter Meghan to her freshmen orientation at The College of the Holy Cross in Worcester, Massachusetts. While there, we went to a lecture titled, *How to communicate with your child by using the Internet!* The purpose of the lecture was to show the parents how quickly the college was moving down the Information Superhighway. The professor who was giving the lecture had a Ph.D. in Computer Science and was in charge of the department. He sat during his talk in front of a personal computer that was connected to a LCD device that sat on the deck of an overhead projector. The deal was that anything he saw on the computer screen would appear simultaneously on the LCD device. The overhead projector would treat this LCD image as though it were an overhead slide transparency and project the LCD image on the screen while the professor spoke.

Wow!

Anyway, that was his plan.

He was using Microsoft's PowerPoint software and he had obviously spent a good deal of time putting together images that moved and swirled and danced at the tap of a mouse button. It was all very impressive.

He sat and boasted of how very advanced the college was and how smart our children were going to be in just four short years, how prepared they'd be to take their place in the 21st Century. He made it through the first five computer-generated images unscathed, and it was truly a wonder to behold.

But then things began to go awry.

His computer did what computers are *prone* to do – that being freeze and die at the *worst* possible moment. He was suddenly projecting an image that read, "This program has performed an illegal operation and will be shut down."

And it was!

He had no back-up slides, of course, because he was a *true* believer in high-tech stuff. Technology would *never* let down a Ph.D. professor who was in charge of the whole department, would it?

Sure it would!

And it did.

And all he had left before him was several thousand dollars worth of hardware and software that refused to cooperate, and a big bunch of parents who were each laying out thirty grand a year for what was in *this* guy's head.

Which didn't look like much just then.

Now, as a fellow teacher, I have to tell you that my heart was bleeding for this poor fella, but there was *nothing* anyone could do to help him just then, and that made me decide there that high-tech was *not* for me. I had been through fires, floods, fights, crazed dogs, crows, low ceilings, locked parking garages, night clerks, and Ray Combs. I knew that *anything* can go wrong and most likely *will* go wrong.

So I was dead set against ever using PowerPoint in my work as a teacher of technicians. I pledged to be forever prepared to go it alone, if need be. Voice only. No projectors, no microphones, no electricity. Look Ma, no hands! You know why?

Because I'd been there.

Simple is good. That was my belief.

The other problem I had with PowerPoint was that most teachers used it to show bullet points of what they were saying. In other words, the slides weren't there for the technicians; they were there for the *teacher*. It was his notes.

And why do I need to look at printed words of what you're saying while you're saying it? It's silly.

I also hated the linear nature of a PP presentation. When you put the thing together you follow each thought with another thought and in a very straight line. If a tech asked a question that had nothing to do with that slide up there, or the next one in the queue, you had to go off topic to answer, and that put the teacher into a one-on-one with the single student. And that left the rest of the students out of the conversation. PP was just like 35-mm slides.

So I hated it.

But the world of teaching kept moving in that direction and people kept asking me why I wasn't following, so I bit the bullet and took a summer course in PowerPoint at my old school, Hofstra University. That's where the professor showed me how to use photos and diagrams instead of words. My eyes were opened to possibilities.

All of the PP presentations I put together afterward contained nothing but photos and diagrams. And these were vague enough that I could shift into any other topic from any point. That technique put me back into the non-linear framework of the overhead slides, but I reached a point where even PP wasn't necessary.

Just before I retired, Ferguson, the nationwide HVAC wholesaler, hired me to go coast to coast with a seminar we called, *What Hydronics Taught Holohan*. This was my last hurrah and I spent all day talking with absolutely no visual aids. I put the PowerPoint behind me and just told stories.

Look ma, no hands.

2015 was my Mariano Rivera year, and a fine way to end a long career of speaking live.

And we sure had fun.

What I loved about that old overhead

I couldn't lose with this thing. It worked with both large and small groups. It was simple. It had hardly any moving parts. It was portable. It wasn't prone to breakdowns. It was a hard-working, blue-collar tool. If a technician asked a question that words alone can't answer, I could make a sketch right there on the spot.

And I loved that I never had to turn my back to the audience. I would just glance down at the deck of the overhead to see what was on the screen behind me. It was like looking in a rear-view mirror. I could look right at the technicians while they're looking at both the enlarged drawing on the screen to my rear, and me. I could point to something on the screen simply by touching the appropriate place on the overhead transparency slide with the tip of my pen. I never needed to turn around, unless I feel like it.

I could also use the overhead projector to direct the group's attention from myself to the slide that I'm showing. I'd flick the projector off when I was done with a particular slide, even if I was going to show another slide in just a few moments. By turning off the projector, I was making the technicians look at me again. It's a subtle thing, but it worked well. The technicians' attention went from me to the slide and back to me again. It was yet another way to keep them awake and aware – and I never had to turn off the room lights!

I'd position the screen so that it was directly behind me. This also applies to PowerPoint. Some teachers like to put the screen in the corner of the room and project at a 45-degree angle, but I prefer having it behind me so that I'm able to move out of the way of the projected image. You have to picture this in your mind's eye to get the effect I'm talking about. I'd be speaking to the technicians, with no picture behind me. They'd be looking right at me. I'd turn on the projector and their eyes will move from me to the screen, which is directly behind me. I'd move a bit to my left (their right) to make sure the people sitting to my left had a good view of the screen. I'd continue to talk as I did this. By moving out of the way, I was directing their attention even more toward the screen, but they could still see me. When I finished with the slide, I'd move back toward the screen to shut off the projector. My movement toward the overhead projector directed their attention away from the screen and back toward me, which is *exactly* where I wanted them to look.

If I had placed the screen in the corner of the room, they would be turning their heads to see the image. I just wanted them to move their eyes, not turn their heads, and that's why I kept the screen behind me. Imagine looking at more than 100 slides during the day. If you had to turn your head back and forth for each one, you'd feel as if you were watching a tennis match. It's tiring, especially when you're not used to sitting still all day long.

I loved those simple machines.

I know you can't hear this, but . . .

In 1998, our twin daughters were seniors in high school and I took Colleen and Erin (Erin now owns HeatingHelp.com) to visit yet another big fancy college. There were over 200 parents and prospective students in this huge auditorium. We were all there to learn more about this fabulous institution from the Admissions staff. They had a lectern set up with a microphone and speakers that would have made Metallica proud.

All was in readiness.

This guy in a suit walks up to the lectern, smiles a big Welcome to Our College smile, and then, for some bizarre reason, scowls at the microphone. "I'm not going to use *this* thing," he says. He then walks around to the front of lectern and proceeds to mumble for the next 45 minutes to the people in the first three rows.

Why wouldn't this guy use the microphone?

I figure he wouldn't use it because he thought that by being unplugged, he would make the meeting more *personal*.

And you know what? It *was* personal. The conversation that was taking place between the Admissions guy and the 20 or so people who could hear him looked *wonderfully* personal. But as for the rest of us middle-aged, hard-of-hearing parents, well, we just looked at each other and said, "What did he say?"

And this is the man who wants me to give him my two daughters for the next four years – along with about a quarter of a million dollars.

Picture me at the end of the first semester when the Holohan twins return from the University of Permanent Debt.

Me: "What did you learn this semester, girls?"

Them: "Not much, Dad. We couldn't hear a thing. They're all a bunch of mumblers up there."

Sort of warms your heart, doesn't it?

I won't be here that long!

I speak to pretty big groups and that means that if I want them to hear me I HAVE TO USE A MICROPHONE. Common sense, right? I mean THAT'S WHY GOD GAVE US THE MICROPHONE, isn't it? So we can *use* it?

But a lot of people aren't comfortable using this important tool. Personally, I'd like to have had one that I could have use around our house. A real *big* one with heavy-metal speakers and an eight-cylinder amplifier. That would be glorious!

Maybe then my daughters would have listened to me?

Now here's something that's always amazed me. An association hires me to speak to a big group of technicians. We've got maybe 200 people in the room. It's a *wonderful* meeting room and I've asked for a microphone that clips to my shirt, which the A/V folks have cheerfully provided.

Someone who is in charge of the association's Education Committee wants to introduce me and get in some nice words about all the good things the association does for its members. I think that's terrific. I *encourage* that sort of thing. I want this group to thrive so that they can hire me again and pay me the big bucks, which I will then forward to the University of Mumblers.

Anyway, the guy walks up to the front of the room and I try to hand him the microphone that's clipped to my shirt. "No, that's okay, Dan," he says. "I don't like those things. Besides, I'm not going to be here that long." He then proceeds to try to communicate with a group that is spread out across an acre of meeting room. The guys in the last row are sitting in Nebraska. You can see by their strained faces and the hands they hold cupped behind their ears that they can't hear a word this guy is saying. "Can you all hear me in the back?" he shouts. The people in the back shout back, "NO!" and shake their heads sadly. The guy doing the introduction smiles weakly and shouts, "Well, that's okay. I won't be here that long!"

They *always* say that. It's as if they were all raised in the same family. The guy then proceeds to scream at the top of his lungs for at least ten agonizing minutes. The people in the back look at each other and whisper, "What did he say?"

Meanwhile, there's a perfectly good microphone within arm's reach of this knucklehead.

Why won't he use the microphone?

He doesn't think he *needs* it. Besides, he's not going to be here that long.

HE'D RATHER SCREAM!

Does all of this make sense to you? It happened to me just about *every* time I worked with an association. It's one of life's great mysteries.

There are mumblers, and there are screamers. And there are unused, unloved, *lonely* microphones attached to huge speakers.

They're right there.

There...

Oh well.

What you ought to know about microphones

Okay, here's the deal. If you want to be heard, you use the stinking microphone. It's that simple.

Okay?

And with that said, let me tell you about your choices.

Personally, I'm a lavaliere man. A lavaliere microphone is one of those tiny ones that clip to your collar and leave your hands free. I like to have my hands free for several reasons. First, I need to hold the remote for the PowerPoint (it's also a laser pointer). I don't want to have to hold a microphone while I'm pointing. Secondly, I like to flail my arms and lavaliere mikes are very flail-friendly.

They come with and without wires. There are pros and cons to each. The wired lavalieres generally have a better sound quality, but I usually wind up tripping over the cord because I am clumsy. The audience loves this, but it's tough on me.

With the wireless lavalieres, you *definitely* get what you pay for. They range from the cheap, scratchy-sounding Radio Shack sets to the mellow, Charlton Heston As Moses systems you'll find in the better hotel chains. You're freer to move around with a wireless lavaliere, but these units are also more subject to interference if you're near an airport (*lots* of hotels are near airports).

Also, if you're using a wireless lavaliere, please turn it off before heading for the bathroom. The range of those things is pretty impressive. I've been caught by this more than once. I'll have three or four cups of coffee, talk for two hours, call for a break, and run for the nearest urinal. When I get back, everyone will be smiling at me. "*Good one, Dan!*" one of the technicians shouts. "We thought the water main broke!"

I remember going to a seminar once where the speaker left his wireless microphone on during a break. He got caught talking to a colleague about "that idiot in the front row that keeps asking stupid questions." The "idiot" heard him loud and clear. So did everyone else in the big auditorium.

And you were wondering how a fight can break out at a seminar?

If you're using a wireless microphone make sure the battery (usually a 9-volt) is fresh. And if you're going to speak for more than three hours, have a spare battery available. These things suck up lots of power, and when the battery gets weak, the sound gets very ragged. You may not be able to hear this when it happens because you'll be speaking. Ask your audience to let you know if the sound isn't right for them. (I also make it a point to ask them about the temperature in the room during the course of the day. Remember, they're sitting still; you're moving around. They're more sensitive to the room temperature than you are.)

If you're teaching in a hotel meeting room make sure you try out the microphone *before* you begin your presentation. Go over all the technical aspects of the system with the hotel staff. Find out where the volume control knob is. Move around the room and stand under the speakers if they're mounted in the ceiling. Make sure your proximity to the speakers doesn't cause the system to squawk. If they have portable speakers set up on tripods in the front of the room, move out in front of them while wearing the microphone. This can often cause the speakers to squawk and it's better to find this out *before* your meeting than during your meeting. Get the name of the person in charge of A/V matters for the hotel and find out how to reach him during the day, just in case something doesn't work as it should.

Hand-held microphones make you look like Jerry Springer and that's your call if you don't mind having one hand occupied. A lot of teachers who aspire to be preachers or lounge singers go for this sort of microphone. The same rules apply to the wired and wireless versions of the hand-held microphone.

And a final thought about wireless mikes. Bring batteries. Have AA, AAA and 9-volts with you. Don't depend on the hotel or catering hall to have these. There's a good chance they won't. Ask me how I know that.

The last choice is the wired, lectern microphone. I don't like to use a lectern in the first place because it limits my movements around the room. It also makes the audience feel as if there's a barrier between them and me. Which there is. It's called the *lectern*. It reinforces that white-collar vs. blue-collar thing, and that's not good for you or the technicians.

Besides, give a teacher a lectern and he's going to hang on it. You've seen that, haven't you? The guy's gripping the lectern like it's the steering wheel of a semi going over a cliff. It makes him look nervous. He's probably *already* nervous. He doesn't need a lectern to help him look even more nervous, does he?

The other thing people feel compelled to do is tap on the lectern microphone and blow into it. "Is this thing *on*?" they'll say. Tap, tap, tap, blow, blow, and blow. "Is it *on*?"

Why do people do that?

"Testing, one, two, three."

And then they start yanking that flexible arm up and down like they're trying to get water from a well. "Is this thing *on*?"

They can do all of this beforehand, can't they? What gives?

Finally, in choosing the lectern microphone you'll probably also be choosing the lectern *light*. These lights, which are supposed to help you see your notes, shine under your chin and give you those spooky Halloween shadows that scare the heck out of little kids every October. You know what I mean? Go stand in the bathroom. Turn off the lights. Hold a lectern light under your chin. Turn it on.

Now *moan*.

Boo!

CHAPTER EIGHT
The "Seminar in a Box"

How to look relaxed

I was getting ready to do a seminar for a wholesaler who had hired me to speak for three hours to 80 of his best customers. We were standing around outside the meeting room, greeting the technicians as they arrived and getting them settled in. "Are you going to give an extemporaneous talk today?" he asked.

"What do you mean?" I said.

"Are you going to talk off the cuff? Do you know what you're going to say, or are you just going to wing it?"

The thought of "winging it" to 80 people for three hours gave me the willies. I started looking around for Knights of Columbus. "No!" I said. "I have the whole thing laid out in a Presentation Book. It's up there by the overhead projector."

"But I've seen you speak before," he said. "I always thought you were just winging it."

"Why do you say that?" I asked.

"Because you always look so *relaxed*. It always looks like you're just having a conversation with the group."

"The only reason I look that way is because I'm *ridiculously* prepared," I said. "I know *exactly* what I'm going to say from one minute to the next, and I know just where I'm going to be at the end of every hour."

"Boy, it never looks it!" he said. "It always looks like you're just up there making it up as you go along. You look so . . . *calm*."

That made me feel pretty good. That's the way you're *supposed* to look when you're prepared. You're supposed to look relaxed. You're supposed to look like you're making it up as you go along. You're supposed to look natural.

That's what comes from preparation.

And here's how to get that way.

Let the Presentation Book guide you

The Presentation Book is really nothing more than a three-ring binder filled with short notes that will cue you and keep you on track. It takes a long time to put together a good one, but once you have it, you can take it on the road and do the same seminar over and over again. After about the third time, you'll probably be at a point where you can tell exactly where you're going to be at a particular time of the day. My seminars became very similar to a theater performance. I knew *exactly* how long it's part would take. I had one-minute stories, two-minute stories, and five-minute stories. I could move any of these around, or drop some of them if we started the seminar late, or had to stop early. Life happens. No one ever knew that they weren't getting the whole presentation. That's the beauty of the Presentation Book. It's incredibly flexible.

Each page of the Presentation Book deals with five or six key points – never more than that. This gives me a way to totally focus on a small portion of the full presentation at a time. I turn the page and it's all there for me. I just have to bring up *these* five points, tell *these* five stories. What comes next is not a concern right now. What comes next is on the next pair of pages. I'll deal with them when I turn the page, but for now, all I have to think about is what's before my eyes. It's total focus.

My Presentation Books remind me of my efforts at marathon running. A marathon is 26.2 grueling miles long, but if you run it one mile at a time it's a heck of a lot easier to handle mentally. When I ran the New York City Marathon I focused on a point just ahead of me and tackled only *that*. I ran over *one* bridge at a time. I ran to *that* tall building at the end of *this* long avenue. When I finished 10 miles, I started to think of the course as a 16.2-mile race rather than as a marathon. When I got to the 20-mile mark, I thought of it as a 10K race. I ran it bit by bit, always aware in the back of my mind that the course was indeed 26.2 miles long, but tackling it in smaller bites nevertheless. Thinking about it that way helped me to reach my goal.

That's what the Presentation Book does for you. It serves up your seminar in bites that are easier to chew. It helps you reach your goal.

Guideposts

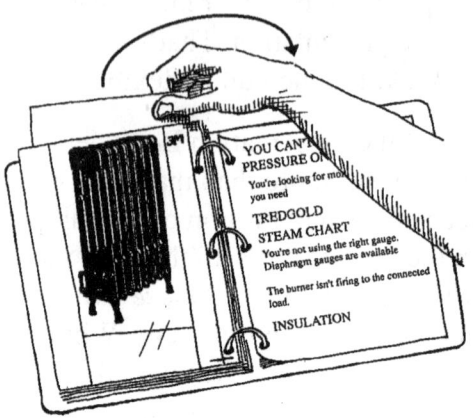

That's the way I think of the notes I make for my Presentation Books – as *guideposts*. They keep me focused and on track from the beginning to the end of my presentation. If I find I have to stray off on a tangent (and that really shouldn't happen if I prepare properly), the notes get me quickly back on track.

I use my computer and laser printer to make my notes. I like to use Microsoft Word's Arial font because it's clean and very easy to read from a distance. I use 24-point type, which is highly readable even with *my* bad eyes, and which allows me to get five or six key points on each page.

Here's an example of the Arial font in 24-point type. Pretty easy to read, eh?

Some teachers like to highlight key points in their notes with a yellow marker. I didn't do this because I was *never* sure what sort of lighting conditions I'd face on my travels. Those yellow highlights tend to disappear under certain types of lighting, especially if you're using a lectern light.

If you need highlights to catch your attention, they just might not be there for you when you need them most.

I used a combination of UPPER- and lower-case letters and standard and **bold** type. When I turned a page, I'd see about five notes for stories or important facts, and five or six **BOLD, UPPER-CASE** cues to get me going. It made everything so easy because It just moved me along from point to point. I couldn't miss! And neither will you.

I'd also use colored paper of various pastel hues for my notes to break the seminar into sections. The change in color when I turned a page *instantly* let me know that it was time for the next topic. I could also see the color change coming when I stepped back from the Presentation Book and glanced down at the edge of the sheets. If you decide to do this, use *pastel* paper and not the bright colors that kids favor for their school projects. Bright colors are too hard on the eyes and you might not be able to see, say, black ink on hot-pink paper if the lights in the room aren't quiet what they should be.

I inserted each page of notes into a Sheet Protector to keep them neat.

When you're making your notes, use as few words as possible. These are supposed to be *cues*, not a manuscript. The words should just key the topic for you and get you started. You know your subject well enough to be able to speak about it. After all, that's why *you're* the teacher! The notes just serve as reminders and keep you moving in the right direction without going off on tangents. They're your *guideposts*. Think of them like the bullet points so many people use in their PowerPoint slides. It's okay to use bullet points in your Presentation Book because you're the only one who will see them. They're not going to compete with your voice.

A final word on the Presentation Book and this is *very* important. Make sure you have a complete copy of *everything* that's in that book, and carry that with you on a flash drive. If you lose the book, you can quickly make a copy. All you need is a computer and a printer, or a nearby Staples. And also store it in the Cloud. You put a lot of time into this Presentation Book. Don't check it in your luggage if you're flying. It may not arrive.

Chain it to your wrist.

Researching your presentation

Okay, let me tell you this right up front. Getting ready for a presentation is hard work. You have to think until it hurts. You have to put in the hours. You have to ask yourself the toughest questions you can imagine. You have to visualize yourself doing the presentation from the opening moments right through to the end. You have to be able to sense how long each portion of your presentation will take. You have to know where you're going to be and at what particular time. It's hard, serious work. Don't save it until the last minute, and don't treat it lightly unless you want to fall flat on your face in front of a group of technicians.

You don't want that to happen, do you?

So *prepare*.

I've written 18 books about various aspects of steam- and hot-water heating. This is a subject that I understand very well, and most folks in my industry consider me to be an expert. Years ago, I put together a full-day seminar for technicians. I called it, *Troubleshooting Steam* and I was going to be speaking for a total of 5½ hours over a day that would begin at 8 AM and end at 3 PM (the balance of the time was for the breaks). I kept track of the hours I spent putting my Presentation Book together for this new seminar. I always kept track of the preparation time because I was curious to see whether I was getting any better at it.

In this case, I was just average. It took me 110 hours to get ready for that 5½-hour seminar. That's a ratio of 20 hours of preparation for each hour of presentation, about average for me. *And this is for a subject that I know inside and out.* If I didn't know the subject, I'd *double* that time.

This is what I mean by hard work. It took me nearly three full weeks of working *exclusively* on this one Presentation Book before I was ready to take it on the road. That included the time it took to outline the day, prepare the notes and the slides, ask the questions I thought the technicians would ask me and then answer them to my own satisfaction, and organize the whole works into a Presentation Book. I did nothing else during that time. It was 110 hours of *total* concentration on this one project.

When I did that seminar for the first time I was *exactly* where I thought I would be at each break, and I finished the day at 3 PM with the very last note in my Presentation Book.

I wasn't *always* able to do this. It takes practice to develop the sense of timing that tells you how much material you'll need and how long each part of your presentation is going to take, but it's not that hard to do. Time yourself when you're going through your presentation and keep notes on how long it takes to tell a particular story or explain a series of technical tidbits. After a while this will become second nature to you.

It also helps a lot if you organize your material into chunks of stories, each that could stand alone as a mini-presentations. Work them into chunks that last about five minutes, ten minutes, and fifteen minutes. This gives you the ability to either add or remove *any* of these chunks, should you have to. Your audience has no idea that you're doing this. All they're seeing is a smooth transition from one subject to the next. I've done this for years and it works every time. I do it because I travel widely and the needs of one group might not be the same as the needs of another group. For instance, when I was preparing the *Troubleshooting Steam* seminar, I deliberately included more material than I could possibly present in 5½ hours. Some of the material was geared more toward commercial systems than residential systems. I'd get a sense of what a group wanted, both before and during the session, and then I would add and remove chunks of material to suit their needs. Again, they had no idea I was doing this. This is where using pastel-colored paper really helps. Commercial subjects can be one color and residential subjects can be another color. If I need to switch, I know *exactly* where to go. During a break, I'd use sticky notes to let me know *not* to tell what was on this page or that page. That gave me flexibility.

That's one of the neat things about the Presentation Book. You can organize each page as a stand-alone unit. If it's 11:45 and you know you're going to break for lunch at noon, you don't want to launch into a portion of your talk that's going to take a half-hour to get through. That would have the technicians looking at their watches at around 12:10 or so, wondering if you're *ever* going to shut up.

But if you've organized your material into five-, ten-, and fifteen-minute chunks you can put the pieces together to fill the time you have to work with. So in this case you could do either a 15-minute section, or a five- and a ten-minute section together. If you didn't have enough time, you could even drop one of the sections and no one would ever know that you did this. By organizing your presentation in this way you gain flexibility and take charge of the timing.

But this is one of the reasons why you have to spend so many hours (a 20:1 ratio in my case) putting that Presentation Book together. It's hard mental work, but it's worth it.

You've already begun your research!

The research you need to do for any presentation doesn't start on a particular day. You should be gathering raw material constantly. The things I'm telling you about in this book took me nearly 50 years to learn. I've kept notes of things that have gone wrong so that I'll remember not to do *that* again! I've also kept notes of things that have gone right (for obvious reasons). When I see someone give a particularly good presentation to technicians, I'll try my best to notice what he's doing that makes him so good. I'll make notes and put those to work for me.

If you gather raw material *constantly* you'll never be at a loss when it's your turn to teach. I could lecture on steam- and hot-water heating because I kept notes and gathered raw material about these subjects for years. I had file cabinets filled with interesting things that I loved to share with technicians. Research doesn't begin on any particular day.

I'll let you in on a trick I've used for years to help me gather raw material. I take a piece of 8½" X 11" paper and fold in half three times. This gives me a folded piece of paper that measures 4¼" X 2¾", or about the size of my palm. It's very easy to write on, and I keep this folded paper in my wallet. I also keep a ballpoint pen in my back pocket no matter where I go. When I get an idea, or when I see or hear something that I might be able to use in a presentation to technicians, I take the paper out of my wallet and make a note to myself. When I fill up one side of the paper, I turn it over and write on the other side. Then I turn it inside out. All in all, a single sheet of plain copier paper gives me 16 panels on which to write notes.

When I fill it up I take it out of my wallet and leave it by my computer. As soon as I get a chance, I type all those notes into an "Idea" file. These became the basis for my books, my magazine articles, and my seminars. I've used this system for many years and it has always served me well. Research doesn't begin on any particular day. *Everything* that you're reading in this book has passed through my wallet at one time or another.

Once you get all your ideas filed away, here's a way that you can make them bloom.

Cluster diagrams

If you're old like me, you may remember when your grammar-school days when your teacher taught you how to make an outline. You began with a main subject, which you labeled with a Roman numeral I. Below this, you listed the items that related to the main subject, giving each a letter of the alphabet. Below the letters, you might have put the numbers 1, 2, 3, 4, and so on.

When you finished with that first subject, you moved on to your second, which you marked with a large Roman numeral II. From there, you continued down the page in a very linear way. If you didn't do it this way, the teacher gave you a bad grade, so you did what you were told.

Outlines and other such methods of organizing things taught you how to think in a straight line. You move from Point A to Point B and so on. You may use this sort of outline when you're putting your presentation together. You'll sit down with a piece of paper and make a list of all the things you'll need to cover. You'll list them in a straight row or perhaps a spreadsheet and you'll be thinking about each point you'll have to make – one point at a time.

The trouble with this is that this is not how your mind works.

Here's what I mean. Stop for a moment and try to think of *just one thing*. Let's make it a grape lollipop. Try to limit all of your thinking to just *that*. A grape lollipop.

Go ahead. Try it.

How'd you do?

It's tough, isn't it? You're trying your best, but your mind wanders away from the grape lollipop, doesn't it? Sure it does. It's nearly impossible to stay focused on a single thing for very long.

You may have thought about a cherry lollipop.

You may have thought about what you're going to do later today.

You may have thought about checking your email.

The phone may have called you away.

You may have thought about the presentation you have to give soon.

Whatever you were thinking about, it was difficult to hold your mind still for very long, wasn't it?

And that's what's wrong with an outline that moves from I, to II, to III, to IV, and so on. This is *not* the way your brain works. Your brain flits around like a butterfly in a field of wildflowers. Linear outlines try to mental butterflies fly straight. They can't do that. It's not natural.

I once read a book called *Writing the Natural Way* by Gabriele Rico (You can get it at Amazon.com). This book changed the way I think, and the way I work. Dr. Rico came up with a new way of drawing an outline. She called it "clustering," because that's what it looks like when you put it on a page. A cluster diagram is nonlinear. It hops all over the page. It's as unorganized as your imagination.

Here's what a cluster diagram of the word "Contractor" might look like (as least as it occurs in my mind).

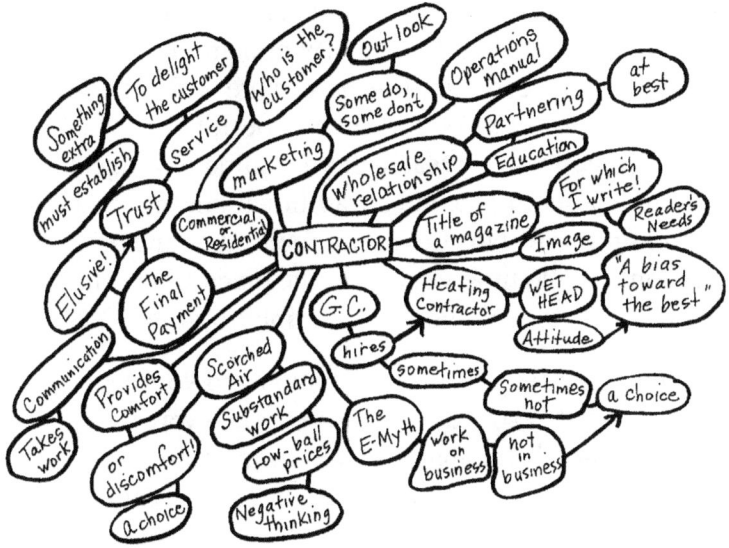

It's the *shape* of the thing that makes it work. It's unstructured and it frees up your thoughts. Clustering gives you a way to catch your creative, nonlinear thoughts. I'll admit that when I first saw it, the pattern seemed really disorganized, but then I learned that that's *exactly* what you need to be to think creatively. Disorganized.

You begin at the center with a core word or phrase. In this case, I used the word "Contractor." From there, you very quickly jot down anything that pops into your mind. And I do mean *anything*. Don't censor your mind. Nothing is out of line here. Just let the ideas flow – even if they seem ridiculous. Let your eyes roam over the cluster as it grows and add *whatever* comes to mind. Don't say, Nah, that's stupid. Just write it down.

Within a few minutes things will start popping out of your brain that you never knew were there. These things will surprise and delight you. You'll remember things from your years of experience with your subject that will bring your presentation to life. This happens because clustering gives you the freedom to mentally hop around. You're not confined to a straight line as you are with a traditional outline. If you get a good idea that doesn't apply to the particular step you've reached, your mind will reject it because it's out of place in a traditional outline. You force your brain to say, No! Let's stay focused on the original question! By the time you get to the place where the good idea belongs, though, you've probably forgotten it.

Clustering frees your imagination and your creativity, and because it is so playful, it gives you a way to dig out a lot of the knowledge that's tucked away deep in your brain. Clustering makes you more creative. Try it right now and you'll see.

Left brain, right brain

The right side of your brain deals with creative thought; the left side is analytical. If you're troubleshooting and you find yourself trying to "think" like water, or electricity, or an internal combustion engine, or whatever, you're using the right side of your brain. Once you figure out what's going on, you sit down and make a list of the material you'll have to get to make the repair. The left side of your brain will take care of that part of the process. The left side is *really* good at adding up numbers and making lists.

There are, of course, nerves that connect the two sides of your brain together, and signals are constantly shooting back and forth at astonishing speeds. Thinking requires both sides of your brain, but in a way, they fight each other. The right side says, *What if?* while the left side is saying, *Now, slow down there!* You need both sides to think a thing through, but clustering keeps you on the right side of your brain a bit longer than you normally would be. The left side keeps trying to drag you back and make you behave "like an adult." *That's* why you might feel that a thought that belongs in your cluster is stupid. The left side of your brain is telling you that it is stupid. It's not. Ignore Lefty while clustering. Just keep jotting down whatever pops into your mind. Trust Righty!

You'll know you're done with your cluster when you just can't write anymore. You'll feel empty. At that point, use the *left* side of your brain to make an orderly list of the items in your cluster diagram. This will bring you back to the sort of linear diagram they taught you to make in grammar school, but it will be *much* deeper and far richer. It will be delicious!

Clustering is *such* a fine technique to use when you're putting together a presentation. All the good stuff comes tumbling out of your brain! Try it and you'll see what I mean.

I keep a large roll of craft paper in my office. I use it to make my cluster diagrams. This book began as a cluster diagram that was two-and-a-half feet high and five feet wide. Every word you're reading sprang from that single diagram.

I wrote 20 books and hundreds of magazine articles. Each began as a cluster diagram. So did every seminar I've ever done. I take the time to cluster because I'm in a hurry. Without the cluster diagram, I wouldn't know where to begin. I'd spend a lot of time staring at a blank computer screen. My diagrams give me a beginning, middle, and an end. They are my mental road maps, and I would truly be lost without them. I'd have writer's block. I don't have time for that, which is why every seminar I've ever put together started as a cluster diagram. It's an amazingly powerful tool, and I hope you put it to good use.

Please put this book down and try it right now while it's fresh in your mind.

Where to go for technical tidbits

The very best place to get interesting information is from your own experiences. That's why it's important for you to gather raw material *constantly*, to write it all down, and to use clusters to get it all out of your head and into your Presentation Book.

Gather it up.

Do it *every* day.

You'll be astonished at how much is already within you.

Next, learn how to research, and not just on the Internet. Go to your public library and wander the stacks. It's peaceful there and you'll focus better without being distracted by Facebook or your email.

If you live near a college or a university, learn how to use their library as well. It's probably bigger and better than your public library. They'll also have the ability to search the stacks at other colleges and universities. Take advantage of their reference librarians. These wonderful people sit at their desks all day long, waiting for a humble teacher of technicians to ask them obscure questions so that they can demonstrate how bright and resourceful they are. Get close to these people; they can make you look great.

Used book stores are also a terrific source of information. This is *especially* true if your technical topic has some neat history behind it. I traveled the country lecturing about old steam- and hot-water heating systems. Without those used bookstores, I wouldn't know half of what I've managed to learn over the years. Walk in, find the proprietor (he's back there behind that tall stack of dusty, yellowed books), and tell him what you're looking for. He'll either point you in the right direction or send you to one of his nearby competitors who just might have what you need. Used-bookstore people are great that way. It's like a fraternity.

Scour manufacturers' literature. Hack through the marketing and get at the technical kernels. If you don't find what you need, call the manufacturer and work your way through the labyrinth until you find some engineer in a back room who's willing to give you all those delicious analogies that will make your presentation sing. The guys in the back rooms are terrific. They generally *love* to talk because they're not often exposed to the people who use their products. They'll also ask *you* for feedback on their products, and that exchange of information will be beneficial to you both.

While you're talking to those engineers, and while you're talking to technicians in the field, gather as many anecdotes as you can. These stories add color and flavor and *life* to your presentation. Talk with old-timers. People in the trades often neglect them or ignore them because old-timers often yammer on and repeat themselves, but these folks have *so* much to share. Embrace their stories and share them with your students.

And use Internet chat rooms. You'll meet like-minded people who are willing to share what they know with you.

We started The Wall at HeatingHelp.com in 1997. Some of the smartest technicians I know ask and answer questions there every day. It's an amazing resource for teachers.

The Internet changed so much in education. Back in the beginning of this book I told you a story about a strange gauge that someone had given me. It read in Atmospheres and in Minutes. The Minutes scale was both upside-down and a mirror image. Remember? I used that gauge to open my seminars because I was fairly certain no one would know what it was for. It convinced the technicians that I was worth listening to.

I didn't tell you what that gauge was used for because I wanted to keep *you* interested. I'll let you in on the secret now, though. You see, I found out what the gauge was used for by searching the long-gone manufacturer on the Internet. I posted the question and a month later I received this reply from John Bevan of the Historical Diving Society in London, England:

"The gauge, once made by Siebe Gorman of England, was part of an oxygen closed-circuit set such as the Amphibian Salvus. The gauge would have been fixed in a low position on the set and out of sight of the wearer. So it was fitted with a lid on a short chain with a mirror on the inside so the wearer could read the gauge. This is why the endurance of the oxygen cylinder is written in mirror English."

How about *that*? Some guy I've never met who lives on the other side of the Atlantic Ocean took the time to share with me some specialized knowledge that had obviously taken him years to acquire.

Please consider that for a moment.

Aren't these exciting times?

Working with a partner?

Okay, let me say this right up front. When it comes to teaching technicians I did *not* play well with others. I never felt comfortable with a team approach to teaching during my days as a manufacturers' rep. I couldn't stand those sessions where I would say something and my partner would then join in with his bit, like the newsreader and the weather forecaster on your local TV station.

And the difficulty was not with the other person; it was with *me*. I would *have to* be in charge of the timing of a class. I would *have to* be able to read the group's needs and shift things one way or another. This was easy to do when I was teaching by myself, but it was *very* difficult to do if I had a partner (or two). How could I get my timing right if the other guy was too long-winded and didn't respect the technicians' time?

One time I was hired to speak to 200 mechanical engineers (all members of a professional society) about steam heating. A fellow I knew (a guy with a *huge* amount of practical experience, but very little teaching experience) asked if he could take about a half-hour of the full-day session. He wanted to share his practical experience with these engineers. He thought they needed more practical experience. He thought they were *much* too theoretical.

"What would you like to speak about?" I asked.

"Oh, just some of my field experiences. I'll tell a few war stories and then sit down. It will blend *really well* with what you're doing, Dan," he promised.

I should have known better, right? But the guy was a buddy and I was a *lot* younger and dumber than I am today.

"Okay," I said finally. "A half-hour, right?"

"That's all I'll need," he said. "A half-hour. *Tops!*"

So he got up there and told one war story. It took him about ten minutes to get through it. I smiled, figuring that things were going well. But then he launched into this diatribe about how blue-collar guys have it *all over* mechanical engineers with their fancy suits and plush offices and how every stinking one of the people in the audience was as dumb as a rock, and it all went downhill from there.

I tried everything I could think of to make him stop, but it was no use. People began to get up and walk out of the seminar.

He kept *speaking*.

I said, "Well, thanks *so* much for sharing that with us. I think we can all learn from each other, but now we should move on . . ."

"I'm not *done* yet, Dan," he shouted. "These suits *need* to hear this." And so he continued, as more and more "suits" headed for the exits. I finally had to physically drag the guy off the podium.

That's why I don't like to share the podium.

Another time (and this was when I was still working for the manufacturers' rep), my boss gave me a guy to work with. I think the boss was afraid of what would happen if I got sick and couldn't make it to the 80 or so seminars I was doing every year. That made sense from a boss's point of view. But the guy that the boss gave me to work with was difficult. Don't get me wrong; he was a great guy and he probably would have made a terrific neighbor, but he kept making the same mistakes over and over again – and they were *technical* mistakes.

At the very first seminar he stood before the class and stated what he believed to be an indisputable fact about some piece of equipment that our company sold. Unfortunately, he was mistaken. Well, actually he was *more* than mistaken. He was as wrong as mortal sin.

I cringed.

A grizzled technician in the audience who installed the stuff for a living challenged the guy on his statement. The technician was, to say the least, upset. My guy stood there and took all sorts of abuse. The other technicians joined in and let my guy know that he had no business being up there, and probably no right to be living on the same planet with them. They then proceeded to throw pizza crusts and beer cans at him.

I sat with my partner afterwards and explained to him where I felt he had gone wrong. We went over the technical aspects of the product and I showed him exactly where he had screwed up. He nodded his head in complete understanding.

The following week we had our second tag-team seminar.

He did it *again*.

And he did it *again* the following week. It got to a point where I knew exactly where and when to duck.

Would you like to hear *why* he kept making the same mistake? He told me it was because he had a note written to himself on the overhead slide's frame. He told me that he *knew* it was wrong but he hadn't had time to change it.

"When I look down and see my notes I just start talking," he said. "I know the facts are wrong, but I just haven't had time to fix it! I get *confused.*"

So there's *another* reason why I don't like to share the podium with anyone.

But that's just me. You may find yourself in the position where you have to work with a partner. That happens a lot in business. So here's some advice.

First, make sure you both agree on the timing. How long will you speak? How about your partner? When will you trade off? Who goes first?

Next, discuss who's going to answer the technicians' questions. Suppose someone asks a question that deals with your partner's material? Will you answer the question, or will you refer it to your partner? It's important that you work this out beforehand because if *you're* going to answer questions about the other guy's material, you had *better* have the same answer he would give if he were standing there up there instead of you.

Don't step on each other's material. If you're supposed to talk about A & B and your partner has C & D as his topics, don't start talking about A & D. You'll steal the other guy's thunder and make him look foolish when he starts repeating everything that you've already said. And besides, if you're going to talk about *his* stuff, who's going to cover *your* stuff?

Make sure you're both in the room for the entire presentation. This is very essential to the continuity of your tag-team performance. Here, let's say your partner goes first and you decide to spend that time on the phone outside in the hallway, or he's off checking his email. Later, when it's your turn to be on the barrel you have no idea what the other guy said. You don't know what questions the technicians asked him. You don't know how he answered those questions (or *if* he answered those questions). You have *no* idea what went on because you were outside in the hallway. You don't even know if they pelted him with beer cans.

If possible, find a partner who has the same style of teaching as you do. If you're humorous and the other guy is dull, the group is going to rise and fall depending on whose turn it is to talk. That's not fair to the audience, and your partner will eventually resent you for being more interesting than he is (if you're the interesting one). If you're the boring one, he'll just flat out *hate* you.

But then on the other hand, office politics often play a part in the pairing, and you may not have any say in this.

And that's yet *another* reason why I chose to work alone. Office politics should *never* play a part in who gets to teach the technicians. The *teachers* should be teaching the technicians. Period.

If a guy can't teach, let him work in the Accounting Department.

But I *will* concede this to you. If you happen to find someone who is compatible, who shares your style of teaching, who understands the technical aspects of the subject as well as you do, who knows how to share, who knows how to bury his ego for a few hours, who knows how to be selfless, who is willing to practice and practice and practice, and who likes pizza and beer, then this can be good for both of you.

But most of the time it's going to be a complete disaster.

CHAPTER NINE
Facing challenges

How to avoid challenges in the first place

- *Never* speak for more than two hours at a time. I say that because that's about the length of a movie. Don't push your luck. No matter how dynamic you are as a teacher, the mind can only retain what the ass can withstand. People need to get up and take a break. They need to go to the bathroom. They may need to smoke. They may need to make a call or check email. They may just need to stretch. Respect that.

- Tell them when the next break will be and then respect that too. If you say there's going to be a coffee break at 10 AM, stop talking *immediately* at 10 AM. Don't keep going until 10:10 AM, or even a minute beyond the time you promised. You are on *their* time now and they will resent you if you try to take it back from them. I don't care that you're in the middle of making an important point. Stop, and continue it later. Besides, if you prepared properly, you shouldn't *be* in the middle of an important point at break time. Right?

- Announce the length of the break before you cut them loose. If you're giving them 15 minutes, announce the break by saying, "Okay, let's take a break. We'll get back together at 10:15 sharp. Is everybody okay with that? Good!"

- When you send them on the first break, let them know where the bathrooms are, and where they can smoke if they have to.

- Have a great story prepared for the first few minutes when they return from the break. Tell them not to be late coming back from the break because they'll miss it. This works *every* time. But make sure you actually *have* a great story. There's another plus to this technique. If you have some latecomers returning from the break, they're not going to miss any important technical information. This is similar to what you did at the start of the meeting. Remember? One of the things I'll do right after a break is to play the Birthday Game, but I'll only do this if the group is larger than 50 people. It goes like this (and it's pretty amazing). You tell them that at least two people in this room filled with strangers share the same birthday. They all start looking at each other and their first impression is that you're wrong. After all, there are 366 possible birthdays, right? So you start by asking anyone with a September birthday to raise his hand. They do and you point at them one at a time, asking them to shout out the date. They do. If you don't get a match, move back to January and take it from there. The reason you should start with September is because September 12, 18, 25, and 26 are the most-common birthdays in America. You know why? Because it's nine months after New Year's Eve. I've never had to go past June when I'm playing this game with a group. It's a statistical certainty that with more than 50 people in a room, at least two of them will have the same birthday. I once had seven matches in a group of 75 people. It's a great way to perk people up. Just get 'em thinking about their birthday!

- Carefully consider where you'll be in your presentation when you take your breaks. You should always try to break on a high note that will create conversation during the break. Try ending with a funny story (you should be thinking about this during your planning stage).

- Avoid the TELL 'EM WHAT YOU'RE GONNA TELL 'EM. TELL 'EM. TELL 'EM WHAT YOU TOLD 'EM method of teaching. It's boring, and this isn't the U.S. Army. It's much more spontaneous and fresh to just swing back to your key points from time to time during your presentation. Repeat the key points, but do it a different way every time, using different examples, coaxing those key points out of different stories. Try to tie the new stuff into the old stuff. That's an effective way to review and it's not at all predictable or boring. You snap your fingers and act surprised. Your eyes light up. You say, "Hey, it just occurred to me that we looked at something very similar to this before. Remember?" And then you recount that story you told earlier. Make all these connections that lace the whole day together.

Those are the basic guidelines that will help you avoid challenges. Now, let's figure that you're having a lousy day. It's *filled* with challenges. And here are the biggest ones you'll probably have to deal with at some point in your life.

Dealing with hecklers

You ever get heckled? It's the ritual that occurs just before they start pelting you with pizza crust and beer cans.

There's probably a good reason *why* they're heckling you. Maybe you've talked past the announced break time. Maybe you're being condescending or disrespectful. Maybe you don't know what you're talking about. Maybe you're being arrogant. Maybe you have no business being up there in the front of the room. Maybe you're just doing a lousy job.

Consider that heckling may be a sincere (but brutal) form of criticism. I've already told you about my experiences with hecklers when I was starting out. I *deserved* all the abuse they gave me, and I learned from it.

So prepare and do a good job. That's the best way I know to disarm hecklers.

Next, don't argue with your audience. If you say something and someone in the audience disagrees, *don't* tell them that they're wrong. Instead, say something like, "Let me restate the point you're making so I can be sure I understand what you're saying." Then you put it in your own words and say, "Is that correct?" The person who is disagreeing will say yes. Then it's your turn again. "That's an interesting point," you say. "Let's explore it." You then do your best to analyze the person's argument, trying to find the place where they've gone wrong. Find that place *together* and get them to see where they're mistaken (this, of course, assumes that they *are* mistaken).

I'll give you an example of what I mean. I teach a seminar about hot-water heating. There's a part where I have to explain the relationship between the pump that circulates the hot water and the tank that holds the air, which gives the heated water a place to expand. I make a drawing of a piping circuit with a pump and a tank. "Suppose we fill this circuit completely full of water, venting all the air, and putting it under pressure," I'll say. I'm showing them a diagram of this, and the technicians are fine so far.

"Okay," I continue, "when the pump comes on, will it pump water into this tank?" I point at the tank with the tip of my pen.

"Yes," a technician says after considering it for a moment.

Now, this isn't possible, as you will see, but I'm *not* about to turn toward that technician and tell him he's wrong. That's the best way I know to create a heckler. I'd much rather he come to the realization on his own. My job is to help him get there.

"This pump is going to put water into that tank?" I say.

"Yes," he answers.

"Are you *sure*?" I say.

"Uh huh."

"This pump over *here* is going to put water into this tank over *there*?"

"Definitely!"

"Okay. But wait just a minute. We only have a certain amount of water to work with, right?" I point to the diagram.

"That's right," the technician agrees.

"So if *that* pump takes some of that water out of *this* pipe over here and puts it into *that* tank over there, what's going to take the place of the water that used to be in the pipe?"

"Air," the technician says immediately.

"Air? Are you sure? Where did the *air* come from?" I ask. "Didn't we vent all the air out of the pipe when we filled the pipe with water?"

"The air came from the water," he says.

I take a long pause to give him a chance to mull over the possibility of that actually happening and then say, "I didn't know you can get air from water. That's pretty cool! That means that you and I could probably breathe under water, doesn't it? All we'd need would be a pump to shove the water out from in front of our faces. We could have all the air we'd need then."

At this point, the technician usually begins to experience an epiphany. But he's not willing to give up yet. He gives me a stubborn look and says, "The pump definitely puts the water in the tank. I've worked on *lots* of these systems."

"But let's think this through," I continue. "If the pump takes water out of the pipe and puts it in the tank, the *only* thing that can be left in the pipe is nothingness – an absolute vacuum, outer space. Is that possible? Can you have a slug of water, a piece of outer space, and another slug of water moving side by side in a pipe?" We're looking at the diagram together as I'm saying this.

The technician finally starts to realize that he's mistaken. "What do you think?" I say, giving him a way out.

"I guess that *can't* happen," he says.

"It can't," I say. "But you know what? When I was first learning this, I believed *exactly* the same thing that you did!"

Fine point there. I'm the teacher, but I also had to learn it. Now it's his turn. We're equals.

And now he trusts me even more.

Do you see what I'm doing? I'm giving him a way out. I'm not backing him into a corner by telling him that he's wrong or that he's dumb. I'm not embarrassing him in front of his peers. I'm not forcing him to defend his position. I'm exploring a technical point *with* him, and together we're coming to a logical conclusion. I'm also disarming any heckling he may have in store for me down the road.

Of course, you have to think all of this through beforehand. That's why it takes 20 hours to get ready for each hour of presentation.

You need to ask yourself the same questions they'll ask you. And to know what those questions are you need to think, and think, and think.

I always expected to get the most heckling when I taught people who worked together. There may be politics going on in that company that I didn't know about. There was probably a Top Dog in the company who was there with us in the room. He didn't want me to appear to know more than he knew. I'll be leaving when I'm done, but *he* has to live with these guys for a long, long time. The guys look up to him, and the worst thing I could do would be to show him up in front of his guys.

So I tried to find out who this guy was right from the start, and then I played to *him* in the beginning of the seminar. I acknowledged him and got him on my side as quickly as possible. I didn't kowtow to him, but I also didn't try to rise high above him. I showed him the respect he deserved. I won him over. And once the group saw that the Top Dog thought I was okay, they became less likely to heckle me as the day went on.

You should do the same, no matter *where* you are. Respect people, especially the older guys.

I often opened in-house meetings by asking all the hecklers to raise their hands. "I just like to know where you guys are so that I can duck," I'd say. The hecklers usually didn't raise their hands, but everyone else would point to them and laugh. "Watch out for Billy over there, Dan. He makes all the teachers who come in here squirm. Billy knows it *all*!"

"That true, Billy?" I'd say, walking over and shaking his hand. "You gonna give me a hard time today? You look like such a nice guy! Hey, I'm a nice guy *too*."

When and if Billy *did* try to give me a hard time, the rest of the group would start laughing and shout, "Hey, Dan, didn't we tell you? He just can't help himself!" And they laugh and laugh.

And disarm Billy.

Worked every time.

Dealing with rudeness

True story. I'm doing a seminar for about 100 technicians and I'm right in the middle of making some big important point when I hear a phone chirp. One of the technicians reaches into his shirt pocket. "Hello?" he says, sticking an index finger in his other ear. "Yeah, howya doin'? Hang on a minute, I can't hear." He puts the phone down and shouts up to me, "Excuse me? Can you keep it down? I got a call."

That was the day I realized that things were going to be just a bit more difficult from then on. Some people are just rude.

So at the start of each session I'll ask the group if there was anyone here who was so important to their business that they couldn't take a vacation day. They'd look at each other, but no one would raise a hand to claim that sort of supreme importance. Even the President of the United States gets to take a vacation day, right?

So I'd probe a bit deeper. "Is there anyone here who gets calls from the office while on vacation? I mean, let's say you're out fishing or at Disney World with your kids. Would you be upset if your office called you and started talking business? Would they even be able to reach you? Suppose you were hooked into a big fish when that phone in your pocket rang. Would you let the fish go so you could take the call?"

Again, they look at each other. No one raises a hand to claim that one either. A few start to laugh at the thought of letting a big fish go in favor of a phone call from the office. Ridiculous!

"I'm just checking, guys," I'd say. "You know why? Because if we have anyone in this room that is *that* supremely important I want to know where he is. And I want to re-seat him near that door over there so that he can step outside when he gets that very important call. That way, he won't disturb the rest of us. But I can see that's not going to be necessary today, because none of us seems to be *that* important. So may I humbly suggest that you give your phones a rest today? That way, we'll be able to relax and focus on all the material we have to cover."

"And think about this. If you were *dead* they'd have to call someone else, wouldn't they? Sure they would! You can't very well answer the phone if you're *dead*, can you? So just for today, *for just one stinking day*, let's all make believe that we're dead. Lord knows you looked that way when I was asking you guys a question a little while ago!"

You know how I can get away with this? Because I say it with a very large smile on my face.

Give it a try; it works most of the time.

But sometimes it doesn't work.

A guy answers the phone in my seminar. He's whispering. I stop talking, but not before saying to the group. "Guys, we have a call. I'm sure it's important. Let's wait until he's done."

Then I stand there and stare at the guy.

The rest of the group sits and stares at the guy.

He says, "I gotta go."

I start talking again.

No one else answers a phone for the rest of the day.

No one.

There are other types of rudeness that you'll probably run into as well. I once had an engineer who *insisted* on lingering on a single point forever. He liked to argue. I figure he thought that this made him look smarter than everyone else in the room. I mentioned this guy earlier when I was telling you about things that can go wrong. The burly contractor sitting next to this engineer decided to punch him in the nose, causing him to stop lingering on that one point.

What we had there was a failure to communicate.

A far *better* way to deal with that situation would be to say, "You're making some good points but I'd rather we discuss them during the next break. That way we can stay on schedule and be fair to everyone else who is here. I'll be able to give you my full attention during the break. Okay?"

If he says, "No!" he'll be turning the whole place against himself (and he might get himself knocked out). And if he does say, "No!" he'll also be the rudest person you'll *ever* meet at a seminar. Just move on in spite of him.

Here's another thing that can *seem* rude but probably isn't. Someone gets up from his seat and stands in the back of the room while you're speaking. This can be disconcerting because you're not sure if it's something that you said. The guy looks like he's going to walk out on you.

Don't worry about it. My guess is the guy has a bad back. He just can't sit still for a long time. He has to get up and move around. He has to stretch a bit. Remember that technicians are not used to sitting still. They have bad backs, knees, and hips in numbers that are disproportionate to the population because of the sort of work they do. I got so used to this standing-in-the-back-of-the-room business that I hardly noticed it after a while.

But then, on the other hand, it may also be a clue that it's time to take a short break.

Let's see, what else? Oh, if you see people chatting with each other while you're speaking don't let it upset you. It may not be rudeness. One guy's probably trying to help another guy understand some point you just made. Stop talking, take a step or two in their direction, and ask them if they need any help. "I see you guys are discussing the point I just made. Was it unclear? I can go over it again in a different way if that would help. Is anyone else confused?" Now step backward, away from them and toward the group.

If they *were* discussing some unclear point, they'll appreciate your offer to go over it again. But if they were just yakking about last night's ballgame, they'll take the hint and shut up.

Dealing with sleepers

I once did a lecture on steam heating to a group of apprentices from a Steamfitters local. We started at 6:30 PM on a workday. We were in a classroom at the union hall and they had those chairs with the attached desks – the kind they make you sit on in high school.

This one apprentice comes in and sits in the back row. He puts his feet up on the chair in front of him, pulls his woolen cap down over his eyes, and goes to sleep. He's sitting there with his hands folded over his ample belly and he's snoring. I look over at the guy who is in charge of the education program for the union. The guy shrugs his shoulders. I let the apprentice sleep. He was probably tired.

You're bound to run into situations like this when you're teaching people who have worked all day. In a group of 100 people I will *always* have one person who is sound asleep for at least a part of the day. I've come to accept this as part of the process of working with hard-working people. Some of us find it nearly impossible to sit still and not fall asleep. I don't take it personally; I just do the best I can with those who are awake.

Those who sleep in class miss stuff. They miss opportunity. They miss *life*. It's on them.

I'm used to this. I do my best to prevent it, but I *never* take it personally.

The first date I had with The Lovely Marianne was memorable. We went to see *The Great White Hope*, which was a film starring a very young, very fit James Earl Jones. I was trying my best to impress her. I even bought popcorn.

Now, there's this big climactic fight scene near the end of *The Great White Hope*. I remember it as a sort of early version of *Rocky*. I was on the edge of my seat with excitement. James Earl Jones was up there on the screen, punching it out with this big palooka and the music was blaring down on us from these great big speakers. Everyone in the place was bouncing up and down.

I looked over at The Lovely Marianne and she was sound asleep.

I decided to propose marriage as soon as possible because I figured she'd be pretty easy to get along with.

And she *has* been for nearly half a century.

You know what I've learned over the years? Some people just fall asleep when they stop moving. Get used to it and please don't take it personally.

But in spite of the occasional sleeper, it's *still* your job to put together a presentation that's interesting enough to keep *most* of the people from dropping into a stupor. That's where the stories and the other techniques we've talked about come in. Be as lively as you can be, and do your very best not to sound like a lullaby.

You ever listen to someone speak in a monotone?

ZZZZZZZZZZZZZZZZ.

Change the volume of your voice *regularly*. DON'T BE AFRAID TO SHOUT SOME OF YOUR WORDS. Get excited about your subject and let your emotions carry you along. If you see someone nodding off, move closer to him as you talk And Raise Your Voice A Bit. This is usually enough to wake them up.

If you have a *serious* sleeper (and here I'm talking about someone who's falling out of his seat), you can also draw the group's attention to him if you do it in a kind way. I've stopped talking completely and tiptoed over to a *serious* sleeper. I'll put my finger to my lips and say, "Shhhhhhhhhhhh." Everyone in the room will start to titter and the sleeper usually wakes up. "How are you doing?" I'll say. He'll get a bit embarrassed and say something about the double shift he just worked. "It's not *me*, is it?" I'll say. "Please tell me it's not *me*!" I'll whine. "I've worked *so* hard to make you happy! My purpose in life is to please you." Then I'll start blubbering. "Oh, *pleeeease* say it's not . . . *me!*"

"It's not you."

"OH, *THANK* YOU!"

Generally, the guy will try a bit harder to stay awake after that.

I've used a water gun in the past. That works too.

I went to the Magic Store and bought a pair of those joke eyeglasses that have the pictures of the wide-open eyes. I'll gently wake up a sleeper and say, "Here, would you mind wearing these? It will make me feel *so* much better."

He'll wear them.

Now, one more word of advice. If a *lot* of people are dropping out of their chairs, you should take that as a clue that this is a good time to take a break.

Or they may be trying to tell you that you're as boring as a phone book.

Are you?

Dealing with questions

First, know that questions are *good* things. Questions mean that the technicians are *listening* to what you have to say, and that they find what you've said provocative.

Next, know that there are *no* stupid questions. No one is born with the answers. The only way to learn is to question. If someone asks you a question that you think is dumb, don't roll your eyes and embarrass the person. Just answer the question as gently as you can.

To get a group going I've often told them the story about the "University of Joe." It goes like this.

When you're young and just starting out in the business, your boss will send you out with some guy named Joe. Now, "Joe" might not be the guy's *actual* name, but you get the gist of what I'm saying, don't you? "Joe" is some old-timer who takes you under his wing and shows you the ropes. You get to carry Joe's toolbox and do all the dirty work. You go for the coffee and do whatever Joe tells you to do. You watch over his shoulder, knowing that Joe is going to teach you *everything* you know. He's not going to teach you everything *he* knows, just everything *you* know.

Then there comes a day during the time that you're matriculating at the University of Joe when you get up the courage to question something that Joe does. "Why do you do it *that* way, Joe?" you might say.

Your Joe then takes a deep breath and turns into Joe Pesci, playing the role of the psycho gangster in *Good Fellas*. He gets right up in your face and says, "*Why* do I do it *that* way? Is *that* what you want to know, kid? IS IT?" You nod nervously. He continues, "Well, I do it *that* way because *that's* the way it's done! Now, you got any *more* stupid questions, sonny?" You shake your head. "No? Good! Now go get me some coffee."

And having completed this course at the University of Joe, you will *never* ask another question as long as you live.

And that's a shame because you'll never learn unless you ask questions. I've found that the Joes of this world act that way because they simply don't have all of the answers.

They react with nastiness because that's their best defense. You're not likely to challenge them again once they've slapped you down.

This is why good teachers *encourage* and *welcome* questions, and try their best to ask the questions of *themselves* while preparing the presentation. A good teacher will say, What would *I* ask if I were brand-new to this industry and wanted to learn as much as possible? I always felt terrific when a technician asked me a question and the very next slide I had prepared contained the answer. That meant that my preparation was very good. I was asking *myself* the question that was on the technician's mind months before I met him. This is one of the reasons why it takes so long to prepare a good presentation. You have to think through the minds of your audience, and you have to ask yourself all the *basic* questions and all the *tough* questions.

Having been taught by some guy named Joe, most technicians are going to be *especially* reluctant to ask questions when they're in a group. They're afraid of looking stupid in front of their peers. This is *very* true of groups that work for the same company. Remember that there may be a Top Dog technician in the room. Win him over by acknowledging his experience. Ask his opinion at key times during the day. He'll help you create an atmosphere where the technicians won't be as afraid to ask their questions.

And please don't be afraid of being too simple with your answers. Those in the know will see the simplicity of your answers as a review and feel even smarter. Those who are *not* in the know will learn the facts for the first time and *really* appreciate the simplicity of your explanation. For instance, I've often described British thermal units as little men with bowler hats and trench coats (*British* thermal units, right?) who live in the boiler and work in the radiators. They commute to work by riding the flow of water through the pipes like passengers on a train. The more British thermal units you have, the bigger the pipes have to be. The bigger the boiler, too. And the radiators as well!

Sounds childish, I know, but it's so simple and so visual that it usually works. Technicians love this sort of imagery.

If it helps me get my message across, it's good, no matter how silly. In fact, the sillier the better.

Invite questions at *any* time. However, first explain that the technicians should ask *only* those questions for which you have *answers*. That always gets a laugh. And if you happen to have the answer, then tell them that is a VERY good question.

If the question relates to the next item in your Presentation Book, then that is a *great* question.

And finally, if the question is one for which you have a slide, well, then that's a *brilliant* question!

Seriously, though, if you're well organized and prepared you really shouldn't get that many questions. You've asked yourself all the important questions during your preparation phase. You've thought through things in a logical order. You've put yourself in the minds of the technicians. You've considered their concerns. You've remembered back to the time when you didn't fully understand the things that you so easily teach today. You've pretended that you're teaching a younger *you*. You've put it all together in a logical order in your Presentation Book. You've answered the questions before they've asked them.

And because you've done all of this, they probably won't *need* to ask.

When someone does ask a question, however, make sure you rephrase it for the group. This is especially important if the group is large. Remember that you have a microphone but the person asking the question doesn't. *Rephrase* the question; don't just repeat it. By rephrasing it you'll be able to put it into the context of what you were speaking about. You'll be able to connect the *relevance* of the question to the points you were making.

For instance, suppose you're talking about how an air conditioning system works. A young technician raises his hand and asks you what a "ton" means, as it relates to air-conditioning. You can say, "What's a ton? It's the amount of heat absorbed in melting a ton of ice in twenty-four hours." By doing this, you would just be *repeating* the guy's question. A better way is to *rephrase* his question into a statement, and then use that statement to lead into your answer. For example, you might say, "You're asking what a ton is as it relates to air conditioning, right? That's a *really* good question because the 'ton' is a term we use all the time, but a lot of guys in the business don't really know what it means. We use it to measure the amount of cooling power an air-conditioning system has. It goes way back to the early days when they used to saw big blocks of ice out of a lake or a river during the winter and then store in ice houses for the summer months. This was in the days before modern refrigeration. Here's how it came to be . . ."

See the difference? It pays to rephrase because it gives you an opportunity to work in other facts and add color and life to your answer. It's also a good way to move yourself forward to the next point you were going to make.

No one will ever resent you for giving them *more* information than they asked for.

But sometimes you're just not going to have the answer. And that brings me to a painful memory.

Every now and then you will run across a technician who will ask you a question so bizarre that it will mess up your mind for years to come. There was such a technician living in my home state of New York. He *always* came to my seminars when I was in his area. He was very supportive and a wonderfully sincere guy. I appreciated his eagerness to learn, but his mind worked in mysterious ways, and it came out in the questions he asked me. Here's what I mean. This is the actual dialogue from one of our go-arounds.

Me: So with thermostatic radiator traps, we have to allow for a drop in temperature of about ten degrees before the trap will release the condensate. Do you have any questions?

Him: Yes, I have a question.

Me: Go ahead.

Him: Did Delta Faucet run any commercials during the last Super Bowl?

Me: "Huh?"

You want to know what that does to you? Imagine you're going about 25 miles per hour on a bicycle. You race past this guy who's standing by the side of the road. He casually steps out into the road and gives you a sideways shove just as you go roaring by. You wind up in the ditch. *That's* what it does to you.

Would you like to hear another question he once asked me? How does this one grab you?

Me: It's *so* important to size pressure-reducing valves to the load, not to the size of the pipe. If you go by the pipe size you'll *definitely* oversize the valve. There is *never* a case where the valve and the pipe should be the same size. If you take the lazy approach and use the pipe size, you'll add *considerably* to the cost of the valve. On top of this, the valve will fail in no time at all from a type of erosion called wiredrawing. Got it? Great! Now, do you have *any* questions about this? It's *really* important that you understand all of this. Questions?"

Him: Yeah, Dan, I have a question.

Me: Yes!

Him: Why do they put those little stickers on the fruit? I mean, do they *have to* put them on *every* piece. It's *ridiculous*! You have to pick off each and every one otherwise they'll get stuck in your teeth. You know what I mean?

He makes little picking motions with his fingers. I lay there dumbfounded, on the side of the road in the ditch, my bicycle wheels spinning drunkenly.

Him: I *hate* that. The little *stickers*, Dan? Do you have *any* idea why they do that? *Why*, Dan? *Why*?"

Me: ?

And the thing is he *honestly* isn't trying to bust chops. I've known this guy for years. He's just curious about *everything*. He thinks differently. He's *way* out there. His mind is not in the classroom with us mere mortals. He is . . . of *another* place.

So be careful because he may be in *your* class someday.

CHAPTER TEN
The meeting place

Finding the place that's right for you

Chances are your meeting is going to be in a hotel. Hotels are used to handling meetings and they're all over the country. Most hotels can easily handle 75 people, seated comfortably in a classroom setting. If your group is going be larger than that, finding a suitable hotel becomes more of a challenge.

Hotels that are located outside of big cities are generally easy to book and to deal with. They're usually *very* happy to get your business. If you're looking to hold a meeting at a hotel in midtown Manhattan (or any other big city), however, you're going to pay a *lot* more, and you'll probably have to book the place six or more months in advance. Move the meeting to the suburbs and things get a *lot* simpler. Also, the parking is usually free in the suburbs. So give a lot of thought to where you *really* need to be.

Now, have you ever noticed that most of the time in life you get what you pay for? Well, that's also true with hotels. I've had experience with most of the major hotel chains in the United States and I've been both delighted and disappointed. When it comes to catering to meetings, I've learned that there is a hierarchy in the hotel business. If I'm trying to book a seminar in some city I'll find out what hotels are available and then I'll work my way down this list (and in this order):

1. Marriott
2. Crowne Plaza
3. Embassy Suites
4. Red Lion
5. Hilton
6. Sheraton
7. Ramada
8. Holiday Inn
9. Best Western
10. Days Inn

Marriott is by far the finest hotel chain when it comes to meetings. They are used to dealing with business people, and they fall all over themselves to please you. I can't think of a single Marriott that has ever disappointed me. They are superb.

As you go down that list everything gets cheaper, and the service and facilities get progressively worse. By the time you get to the Days Inn *anything* can happen – and it probably will!

You pays your money and you takes your chances!

I once got hired by a manufacturers' rep to do a seminar at a Days Inn in a small city. They had arranged with the folks at the Days Inn for a buffet lunch, and they had agreed to a per-person charge for same.

Now, I'm *always* the last person on line at lunch because I want to make sure the hotel staff is taking good care of the guests. I just stand in the background and watch. In this case, only half the people went through the buffet line when the cold cut platters ran out of cold cuts. I found a waitress and asked her if she would please bring out some more meat and cheese for our guests. She returned from the kitchen a moment later with this big sloppy guy in a cook's uniform. He got right in my face and said, "You got some sort of *complaint* here?" I backed up a step and said, "No, there's no *complaint*. We just ran out of cold cuts. We're paying a per-person charge and we've run out of food. Half of our guests have nothing to eat. That's all. Would you please bring us some more food?"

He looks out over the room filled with technicians and glares at those who are eating their sandwiches. "You know why there's not enough food?" he says. "It's because *they* took too much!" He jabs his thumb at the group.

Now, keep in mind that we were paying *per person* for this fabulous buffet. There was nothing in the contract that specified the *size* of the sandwich each technician could make. He thought there should have been, though.

Anyway, he returned about 15 minutes later with a small platter of the fattiest roast beef I have ever seen. And I had this nagging suspicion that he had spit on it.

And this is why I will *always* put the Days Inn at the bottom of my list when it comes to hotels.

Another time, I walked into the lobby of a Best Western. It was 6:30 AM and I politely asked the guy at the front desk if he would take the chains off the door to our meeting room so that I could bring in my stuff and get ready for our meeting. He said he would, so I strolled down the hallway to wait for him, confident that he would be along directly.

Ten minutes later I was still standing in the hallway.

I went back to the front desk to find out why he hadn't shown up with his keys.

"Are you going to open my meeting room?" I asked.

"I can't," he said.

"Why not?" I inquired.

"I can't find the keys," he explained.

"Does anyone else have a spare set of keys?" I queried.

"Yes," he replied.

"And who would that be?" I politely asked.

"That would be the manager," he revealed.

"Is the manager *here*?" I wondered aloud.

"Nope," he said simply, as if that explained all that was wrong with the Universe.

"When will the manager *be* here?" I asked.

"She comes in at nine," he said.

"But my meeting starts at *eight*!" I shouted, turning quickly into a New Yorker.

"I don't know what to tell you," he said, shrugging his shoulders in utter hopelessness.

"I HAVE A CONTRACT!" I shrieked.

"That may be so, but she's got the *keys*," he volleyed back.

"Can't you *call* her on the phone?" I cajoled.

"No *way*! She gets *really* mad when anyone calls her at home. Don't worry, she'll be along directly. Just try to be *patient*, sir." He rolled his eyes toward the ceiling.

And that's when I turned into the Terminator.

They got the door opened, all right. But they had to take it off the hinges to do it.

Seriously.

And this is why I love the Marriott chain. *They have keys.*

Can you stand one more? A company hired me to do a seminar for 35 technicians in New Jersey. At 6 AM I asked the night clerk (that *cursed* breed!) at the Howard Johnson to open my meeting room. He handed me the key to a room and pointed me in the general direction in which said room was to be found. The room was on the second floor of the motel, which seemed *very* strange because it was along the sort of hallway where you expect to find motel rooms. I got to the room that matched the number on the key and opened it.

It *was* a motel room.

They had removed the bed and the dresser and put in 35 folding chairs. The chairs went from wall to wall and back to front. This was in the days when I used to travel with three projectors (overhead, 35-mm slide, and video), that prop wooden boiler I told you about earlier, and a bunch of other stuff.

I stormed down to the night clerk and asked him where the "real" room was.

"That's it," he said. It seems the Howard Johnson was doing some renovations on the "big" meeting room. "You'll just have to do the best you can," he told me.

I'm glad they went out of business, and this is just one more reason why I *love* the Marriott.

But there are exceptions on that list, of course. Every now and then one of the lesser hotel chains delighted me. It all depended on who was running the place at the time. Most of the chain hotels are franchises owned by private corporations. This is why you can have a meeting at a Holiday Inn one year and return the following year to learn that the place is now a Ramada. I've even had an occasional Days Inn that worked out okay. It all depends on the staff and their commitment to quality service.

Sort of like in *your* business, eh?

We used a particular Holiday Inn near Chicago twice and both times the staff was superb. The third time back, though, they were horrible. I asked to speak to the manager who had taken such good care of us on the previous two visits only to be told that she had been promoted to the Regional Office. She deserved the promotion, but her replacement had *ruined* her hotel.

The higher you go on that list, the less chance you'll have of being disappointed or surprised. They are *consistent* at the top of that list. You'll also pay more for that consistency, of course. A Marriott will cost you *at least* 50% more than a Days Inn on any given day – and even more if the Marriott is in a big city. Nevertheless, when any of those top-three hotel chains are available to me, I'll choose them every time. Remember that, as the teacher, you are just *one* leg of that four-legged stool. The other three "legs" are the technicians, your teaching tools, and the setting.

Choose the setting carefully and you'll have better control over the other three legs.

Important things to look for in a hotel

Give a lot of thought to where the place is located if the technicians will be arriving by car. Consider the traffic patterns both in the morning and in the afternoon. Try not to pick a place that's going to force your guests into the jaws of rush-hour traffic. That can only put them in a bad mood and delay the start of your meeting.

If people are going to arrive the night before, or if your meeting is going to last more than one day, arrange for the hotel to provide a block of rooms for sleepover guests. They'll get a break on the price, and you'll also have more pull with the hotel when you're negotiating the price of the meeting package. You can cancel the unused sleeping rooms a few days before the meeting without any penalty, in most cases.

You can often get the meeting room for free, or at a substantial discount, if you're buying enough food, or booking enough sleeping rooms from the hotel.

Ask.

Many of the better hotels offer food packages (usually called "The Executive Break" or something similar). These are worth considering if you're going to have a full-day meeting with coffee breaks and lunch. But make sure you don't order food that's too heavy or you'll be going head to head with the technicians' physiology. It works like this. Right after a human being eats, the blood leaves the brain and travels to the stomach to digest the food. The result?

ZZZZZZZZZZZZZZ.

Keep it light.

I once got hired to do a full-day seminar in Cincinnati. The sponsor decided to order the All-You-Can-Eat, Gorge-Yourself-Into-A-Coma Pasta Bar for lunch. By 1:30 PM, my meeting room looked (and sounded!) like your living room does at 7 PM on Thanksgiving.

If you're not buying food from the hotel, or looking to reserve sleeping rooms, you're going to have a tough time booking a meeting room in advance. The catering staff will tell you that nothing is available, figuring that some group that's willing to spend more money with them on that date will show up. Don't be surprised if a hotel that turned you down calls you later on (about a week before your meeting) to say that they now have space available. That means their gamble didn't pay off and now they're looking to fill the room with *any* group.

When you're booking the space, ask if there is another event scheduled for the same space immediately *after* your class. I'm often descended upon by a horde of hotel people working like maniacs to turn my seminar room into a wedding reception. They have 30 minutes to do this, and they're shoving the technicians who stuck around to ask me questions out the door.

If you're going to be teaching in an unfamiliar area and you need to book a hotel, go to the Meetings & Conventions website (http://www.meetings-conventions.com/meeting-facilities).

Plan a vacation for yourself while you're at it. You'll need it by the time you're done planning your meeting.

Non-hotel meeting places

And that brings us to restaurants and catering halls – also the VFW hall, American Legion hall, Knights of Columbus hall (Yikes!), the local firehouse, a college lecture hall, the movie theater, or whatever. Be creative. You'll be amazed at what's for rent during the slow times. A movie theater, for instance, will often be available for a morning meeting. You get this *really* big screen, Dolby sound system, comfortable seats, plenty of parking, and, if it's in a mall, probably also a food court. It is tough looking up at your audience, though.

University lecture halls are also good places to have meetings during the summer months when the majority of the students are away. You'll usually be able to get food at the cafeteria because the campus is still open for prospective students and their parents who are attending information sessions. They even have microphones (although few actually use them).

If you're looking at a restaurant or a catering hall pay close attention to the height of the ceiling. Look for any columns that might block sight lines. Also, watch out for chandeliers that hang down so low that they'll block the view of the screen. Make sure the lighting is right for your needs. Candlelight may be romantic for an intimate dinner but it's not so pleasant at a seminar. Oh, and know that the controls for the lights in a catering hall are often a half-mile away from the glitzy room in which you'll be having your meeting. And nothing inside that lighting panel is *ever* labeled. I'm serious. There is some old guy named Gus who knows which switch operates which lights, but he doesn't come in until you're done.

If you're renting a hall and you're going to need food, someone will have to bring it in from the outside. Ask the person in charge of renting the hall if they work with a caterer. Most have an arrangement with a local delicatessen or restaurant. It pays to work with the folks they recommend because this caterer will know how to get the food setup on time.

You can often get these halls for less money and they usually don't rush you out the door the moment your meeting ends. That's another plus.

But none of them are the Marriott.

The room set-up

The room you choose will determine the size of the group you can teach. Vice versa as well. Go for comfort above all, especially if your session is going to be longer than two hours.

I've always preferred classroom seating. This is the type of set-up where you have long tables in rows that face the front of the room. It's a great set-up for taking notes. It also gives the technicians a place to put their coffee cups, water glasses, eyeglasses, and, when I was in Virginia, the ever-popular *spit* cups for the temporary storage of the byproducts of tobacco chewing.

Now *there's* a pretty sight!

If you have an option, ask the caterer to place the water pitchers in the back of the room rather than on the tables. That will keep the technicians' derrières from tipping the pitchers of ice water into the laps of the technicians who are already seated.

This, as I mentioned earlier, once started a brawl at a seminar I did in New York.

Start spreading the news.

As to pencils (or pens) and paper, put them on the tables so that the technicians will be able to take notes. I'm constantly amazed at how many technicians will show up at a seminar without paper or a pencil. *Nobody's* memory is that good. Encourage note taking as you go through the day. Remember that the average adult will forget 93% of everything he's taught within 72 hours of your meeting. That's why notes are so important. And know that most good hotels will provide pencils (or pens) and paper for free. All you have to do is ask.

If you're setting things up classroom style, don't put too many big people at one table. Allow about 2½ linear feet for each person. Don't put the rows too close together or people will be climbing over each other when they have to get up to use the facilities. Leave a row up the center of the room and a row up each side as well, if possible. This makes it easier for people to come and go, and it's also important for fire safety. The center aisle also gives you a way to wander into the audience from time to time – if you're using a wireless microphone.

Theater seating is less comfortable than classroom seating. Theater seating is what you'll find at most conventions. It's just row upon row of straight-back chairs with no tables. You can get a lot more people in the room with theater seating than you can with classroom seating. However, with theater seating, there's no place to write, other than on your lap (and a lot of technicians don't actually *have* laps!). There's also no place to put your coffee cup (other than on the floor, which can get messy in a hurry). Theater seating is okay for a short meeting, but I wouldn't use it for any meeting lasting longer than two hours.

The exception, of course, is if you're in a *real* theater. Many hotels have amphitheater rooms (so do colleges and universities). The chairs in these rooms are comfortable and they have little desks that pull up from the sides. They're also set in rows like a theater, with each row higher than the one in front of it. These places are generally *very* nice.

Now and then, a group will hire me and set up the room with round tables, just as if it were a wedding reception. You can get more people in a room set with round tables than you can with a room set classroom style, but some of those people at the round tables are going to have their backs to you all day long. They compensate by turning their chairs, of course, and this sometimes makes it difficult to take notes because it puts them back into a theater-seating arrangement. Those who arrive early get the best seats.

That's true of a lot of things in life, eh?

Little meetings fit in little rooms. Here, you can use a conference table or a round table. This changes the dynamics of the meeting because the technicians are looking at each other, as well as at you. They're picking up facial expressions and body language that can either help you or hurt you, depending on how your day is going.

You can also set up a little room with classroom- or theater seating, of course.

But never try to fit 35 burly technicians into a motel sleeping room.

Trust me; they don't fit.

Whatever size meeting you're having, in whatever place you choose, try to close the drapes to block out the view of the Great Outdoors. You want the technicians to look at *you*, not at what's going out outside. I had to compete with the Pacific Ocean and a Hawaiian beach when I did my seminars in our gorgeous 50th State. There were no drapes in that room. Even *I* had a tough time paying attention to me.

If you can, go to the room the night before your meeting and stand in the front for a while. Then walk around and sit in some of the seats. Imagine that you're a technician in the audience and that you're watching yourself do this *great* presentation.

Now, go back to the front of the room and imagine yourself *giving* that great talk. Think about how everyone will be smiling at you and applauding you at the end. They'll walk up to the front of the room, shake your hand, and sincerely *thank you* for sharing your knowledge with them.

Visualize *success* as you fall asleep that night.

Then wake up early and wow them.

Grub!

Hey, you may have to feed them!

After doing a whole lot of seminars, here's what I've learned about technicians:

First, if possible, have the lunch served in another room. It's good to be able to get up and leave the seminar room for an hour or so. It breaks up the day, and it gets you around any noise the catering people might make while setting up a buffet in the back of your meeting room.

For a full-day meeting (and by that, I mean something that starts at, say, 8 AM and ends at 3 PM) begin with coffee (both decaffeinated and high-octane), tea, and some sort of bread/cake/Danish. Have it ready at least an hour before the start of your meeting because many technicians like to get up in the middle of the night to go to work. They'll show up at your seminar before the crack of dawn and say things like, "Hey! I've got several thousand questions to ask before we get started, and a stack of photographs of oddball things I'd like to show you. And by the way, where's the coffee and donuts?"

So have it all ready for that guy and his brethren.

If you're going to work with a hotel, they're going to offer you the full range of possibilities. A cheap hotel will suggest coffee that tastes like walnut shells, and stale Danish. A yuppie hotel will smugly suggest the EXECUTIVE BUFFET, which includes coffee, tea, seasonal fruit, Natural Nutloaf that looks like the coagulated contents of a bird feeder, healthy pastries (an oxymoron), designer water, fresh-squeezed juices (that goes without saying!), linens, silverware, china plates, cups and saucers, and everything else swanky. The price will make you say ouch.

So let's get back to the essentials: Coffee (regular and decaf). Hot water for tea. Some sort of pastry (like the stuff you get at home).

That's what you should have in the morning at every meeting you schedule, unless it happens to be in beautiful Salt Lake City, Utah. I once set up a meeting there and ordered 12,000 gallons of coffee, only to have a hundred members of the Church of Latter Day Saints show up bright and early to tell me that Mormons don't drink coffee.

I should have known that.

I drank a *lot* of coffee that day.

And please keep in mind while planning your meetings that Jewish people probably won't appreciate the loin of pork sandwiches you're serving for lunch either. In like fashion, Hindus are not going to chow down on that rare roast beef. And then there are the vegetarians.

Be *sensitive*.

If you're planning a break about two hours into your full-day seminar (and you *should*), refresh the coffee, but don't put out any more food. It only makes people sleepy. Lunch is just a couple of hours away. They can wait.

And speaking of lunch, keep it light. Sandwiches and salads work best. If you feed them potato pancakes, dumplings, stuffing, and fettuccine alfredo, chances are good that they'll all be on the floor fifteen minutes after lunch.

If you're having a buffet, ask the caterer to set the buffet line so that people can access it from both sides. This will move the line through in half the time it takes to get everyone served when only one side is accessible. This seems like common sense, but you wouldn't believe how many times I've seen that buffet table pushed up against the wall.

Oh, and if the caterer is serving soup ask them to make it the *last* item on the table. This is one of those fine points that often get missed with hotel catering staffs. Because people generally eat the soup first, most caterers make it the first item on the table.

Now picture this. A technician pours himself a big cup of hot soup, filling it right to the brim because it's free and he doesn't want to miss out on any of the good stuff in life. He will then try to balance this cup of molten chicken lava on a little saucer while he tries to make himself a great big sandwich. He's spilling the hot soup all over himself as he moves down the line. He's whimpering in pain and by the time he gets to the dessert tray (which he also has to pillage *right now*) he only has a half-cup of soup left anyway.

Multiply that by a hundred hungry technicians and you begin to see why it pays to make soup the very last thing on the line.

Nevertheless, I've had caterers argue with me *vehemently* over this soup issue.

"Where are we going to put the *dessert*?" they say.

"Put it first," I answer.

"That's *ridiculous*!" they shout. "Who eats the desert *first*?"

You following this?

Habit is a *tough* thing to break.

If you happen to be teaching engineers, allow extra time for a buffet lunch because engineers are *very* precise when it comes to making sandwiches. They don't actually *make* a sandwich; they *build* a sandwich. The meat and the cheese must align and the mustard or mayonnaise can't extend to the crust. Give 'em an extra 15 minutes for purposes of peculiarities. I'm serious.

And speaking of mayonnaise (and salad dressings), *you* should stay away from these particular condiments. They are *not* worth the risk. Mayonnaise and salad dressing can turn bad in a hurry when left out of the refrigerator for too long. You have no control over this. If the mayo is rotten you will get *very* sick, very fast, and that will put you out of commission for days. I once did a seminar in Elkhart, Indiana where 60% of the technicians got violently ill from bad mayonnaise. It was a good hotel that was having a bad day. It broke my heart when this happened, but I don't know what I could have done to avoid it. These things happen in the real world.

Learn to like mustard, oil, and vinegar.

And *always* be the last person to eat. This has nothing to do with food poisoning (hey, *you* taste it and I'll watch). It has to do with courtesy. Make sure your guests are fed and settled down before you take care of yourself.

Go over the break times and the lunch times with the caterer the day before your meeting, and then again on the morning of your meeting. Make sure everyone is in agreement on what's supposed to be ready and at what time so that when you call for a break, the technicians can walk out of the room and find everything waiting for them.

Have these times spelled out in your contract if you're working with a hotel or catering hall. Have a copy of the contract with you.

If you're planning a break in the middle of the afternoon, serve soft drinks and coffee. You can skip the food because they'll still be digesting their lunch. There's no reason to send even *more* blood to their bellies, is there?

ZZZZZZZZZZ.

Timing is everything in life

Now a word to the wise – for what it's worth. As with the food you pick, be *very* sensitive to the dates you choose for your meetings. For instance, I am a good Catholic boy, but I would *never* schedule a seminar on a day that any other religious group considers sacred. For instance, I never once did a seminar on Yom Kippur, the most holy day on the Jewish calendar. If a group tried to hire me on that day (and many have), I would say no because it would offend my Jewish friends. It's disrespectful.

I never did a seminar on Good Friday either.

For what it's worth.

Dan Holohan Associates' hotel specifications

When we sponsored a series of seminars we generally called each of the hotels about four months ahead of time and asked if they had room available on the day that we had in mind. If space was available, we'd then send them this specification sheet, which we came up with after years of dealing with disasters. Feel free to use it as is, or adapt it to suit your own particular needs.

Good morning!

Here is a list of the elements we would need to conduct a successful seminar for 75 people at your hotel. Our speaker uses PowerPoint throughout the day so both the size and shape of the room are crucial. The people attending the seminar must be able to see the image on the screen at all times.

Thanks for taking the time to review our needs. Please let us know if you can accommodate us.

Room requirements: We prefer a ground-floor location. The room must be at least 2,000 square feet in size with no interior columns that might obstruct lines of sight. We prefer a room that is more square than rectangular since we've found that this gives our attendees the best possible view of the projection screen.

We require a minimum of 12-foot clearance from the floor to the ceiling's lowest point. Please advise us if the room has hanging chandeliers or partitions that might obstruct any attendee's view of the projection screen.

The room-lighting controls should be easily accessible from within the room.

So that we may be able to quickly contact the hotel staff, should the need arise, we require a house phone either in, or very near, the meeting room. A member of the hotel staff should be available during the day to adjust the room temperature if necessary. Someone from the hotel should also be available to deal with any mechanical-equipment and audio/visual challenges that might arise throughout the day.

Set-up: We'd like the room set classroom-style for 75 large adults without crowding. Please allow 2-1/2 linear feet between each chair. Allow for a center aisle, and an aisle at each side, if possible.

Provide a projection screen suitable for the room size, but not smaller than 8' × 8'. The screen should extend as close as possible to the ceiling and be fully visible from all the classroom seats. Position the screen at the center of the room's front wall.

Provide a long table for the speaker's computer and projector. Set the table approximately 10 feet in front of the projection screen.

Provide a lavaliere microphone for the speaker. If available, we'd prefer a wireless unit. Provide a spare battery for the microphone. The audio speakers should be part of a balanced house system, not contained within a portable lectern.

The speaker will not need a lectern or a chair.

Provide a pitcher of water (no ice) with a lemon, and a glass for the speaker.

Provide four, skirted, eight-foot-long display tables set in the rear of the room.

Provide a skirted, eight-foot-long registration table with one chair directly outside the room's main entrance, which should be at the rear of the meeting room.

Provide water pitchers and glasses for the attendees on a table at the back of the room.

Set-up must be completed, and the room fully prepared, by 6:30 AM on the day of the seminar.

Time frame: Registration begins at 7 AM. Our meeting starts at 8 AM. Our meeting concludes at 3 PM. We'll have a 15-minute break at 10 AM. We'll break for lunch between Noon and 1 PM.

Catering requirements: As the attendees arrive at 7 AM, we'll want to offer them coffee (regular and decaffeinated), tea, and pastries.

We'd like you to refresh the coffee and tea at 9:45 AM for the 10 AM break. Leave out any pastries not eaten during the 7 AM break.

We'll have a buffet-style lunch at Noon. To minimize our attendees' time on the buffet line we'd like you to position the buffet table so that a line of people can access it from both sides. If soup is offered as part of the buffet, please position the tureen *after* the sandwiches so the attendees will pick it up last.

Sleeping rooms: Our speaker will require a nonsmoking room with a king bed the night before the meeting, and possibly on additional nights as well, depending on the date of the meeting.

Please block out ten additional sleeping rooms for possible use by the seminar attendees. Please let us know your policy for releasing the block of rooms, should the attendees choose not to reserve them.

Noise: Please let us know of any other event you've scheduled on the day of our seminar that may be distracting to our speaker and attendees. Among these events might be corporate pep rallies, meetings incorporating musical groups or loud recorded music, and/or meetings during which loud mechanical or A/V equipment will be used.

In addition, please let us know if the hotel or the hotel grounds are scheduled to be under construction or undergoing major repair work on the day of our meeting.

Vehicle parking: If there is a daily charge for parking, please let us know what it is, and whether you will either waive it or offer our attendees a discount.

Posting: Please post our meeting as "Dan Holohan Seminar."

Payment: We'd like to pay your invoice at the conclusion of the meeting (and any prior required deposit) with an American Express card.

This specification has helped us avoid *so* many misunderstandings with hotels. The catering staffs we've dealt with have told us that *very* few groups give them such detailed specs. They really appreciate what we've sent them because it helps avoid any misunderstandings and it gives them the option to tell us right up front whether or not they can meet our needs.

This spec follows the same philosophy as the Presentation Book. Plan in advance. Think it all through. Prepare well.

Do this and everything should go smoothly – *if* you're working with a good hotel.

CHAPTER ELEVEN
Happy endings

Knowing when to stop

How do you know when to stop? It's pretty simple. You stop when you *said* you were going to stop. Don't go beyond your announced stopping time. If you do, you'll be on *their* time, not yours. If you didn't finish by the end of the day, that's *tough*. Just shut up. Oh, I know you're irresistible, wonderful, and good looking, but those technicians have places to go and things to do. Their time is just as valuable as yours.

So do what you said you were going to do.

Stop.

When you're putting your Presentation Book together, save one of your best stories for the very end. Make that story positively *inspirational*. You want to finish on the highest note you can possibly reach.

Your ending might be a call to arms. Give a lot of thought to this. What action do you want the technicians to take immediately after the seminar? Do you want them to sign up for another seminar? Perhaps a more advanced one? Do you want them to read certain books, or listen to (or watch) certain tapes? Do you want to challenge them to do something specific? Perhaps suggest something new to the customers? Sell something? Cut down on repeat calls? Work more closely with each other and with management?

Will you be meeting with them again? Do you want them to consider something or prepare something by that time? How should they go about this?

What is your call to arms?

Spend at least a few moments at the end of your presentation thanking them for taking the time to hear you out, and for considering what you've had to say to them. Let them know how they can get in touch with you in the future if they need to.

And make sure you stick around at the end for questions. There will always be those who don't want to ask their questions in front of the group. Allow at least a half-hour at the end of your seminar for private questions, if at all possible.

How did you do?

Some teachers like to use an evaluation sheet to find out how they did. If you work for a company, your boss may require that you do this. In any case, if you use an evaluation sheet have it serve a *specific* purpose. The *best* purpose I know of is to learn how you can make the seminar even better next time. Don't produce an evaluation sheet for the purpose of stroking your ego. We *all* like to be told that we're wonderful, but that's *not* what an evaluation sheet is for. The evaluation sheet is there to make you *more* wonderful the next time around. It's a *tool*.

Phrase the questions in a way that will get you the information you're after. Spend a lot of time thinking about these questions. What do you want to know? What will help you improve, to serve your audience better next time? Make yourself a cluster diagram when you're putting together this list.

Leave a space for the technician's name, but also explain at the top of the sheet that he can be anonymous, if he feels more comfortable with that. This encourages the technicians to be brutally honest with you, and this is *especially* important if they happen to work for you.

Start with a series of questions that the technicians can answer by circling a number between 1 and 5. Clearly explain that on this scale, 1 is the worst and 5 is the best. Someone may give you a sincere evaluation, wanting to let you know that they were *very* pleased, but if they get the numbering system backwards the message you'll get will be just the opposite of what they *meant* to write.

Here's a list of some of things I would be interested in learning from any group of technicians that I taught:

- Did I do a good job of explaining the subject today?
- Were my explanations clear and understandable?
- Was I talking over your head?
- Did you understand the terms I used?
- Did you enjoy my use of stories today?
- How would you rate my overall presentation?

- How would you rate the coffee breaks?
- How would you rate the lunch?
- Were the breaks spaced well?
- Did you have enough time during the breaks to take care of your personal needs?
- Was the room we used a good one?
- Were the chairs comfortable?
- Was the temperature right?
- Was the lighting sufficient?
- Could you hear me all right?
- Could you see the slides on the screen?
- Were the slides understandable?

Notice the way I'm asking the questions in a way that's one on one. I'm not saying, "Did the speaker do a good job?" I'm making it personal. "Did *I* do a good job?" I just spent the whole day building a personal relationship with these people. I'm not about to start hiding behind the passive voice at the end of the day. *I* want to hear from *you*. What *you* have to say is important to *me*. This is the right way to end the day.

Be sure to include a few questions in the evaluation sheet that encourage written comments as well. I always find these to be the most valuable of all. The technicians who remain anonymous will give you some of the *most* useful written comments.

You might ask them to:

- Please list the two most valuable things that you learned today.

The answers to this one are liable to surprise you. Their input might even cause you to redirect the seminar the next time around so that you spend more time on the areas that have made such a positive impression on them.

Here's another good one:

- Please list one or more ways that you think I can improve this seminar.

Expect to hear a lot of silly answers to this one. I've gotten comments such as "Free beer," and "Charge less money!" But I've also gotten many thoughtful comments that have helped me to improve both my skills as a teacher and the technical content of my presentations.

Finally, thank them *sincerely* for coming to the meeting. Always remember that you're there for each other. You and the technicians are two legs of that four-legged stool.

Be humble.

Certificates?

Certificates of completion mean a *lot* to some technicians. They'll take those certificates home and hang them on the wall as symbols of their achievement. They're rightly proud of what they've accomplished under your tutelage. They should be. So should you. You've worked well together.

Certificates are not expensive and you can make them yourself. Search Certificate Software on the Internet and take your choice. Print them on quality paper that won't yellow with age.

If you decide to award certificates, do it either on the day of the seminar or follow up within several days by mail. Make sure you've spelled each person's name correctly.

If you're giving the certificates out on the day of the seminar and the group is large, have someone lay out the certificates in alphabetical order on the registration table just outside your meeting room.

Congratulate the technicians at the end of the day when you're wrapping things up and tell them they can pick up their certificates on their way out. Don't stand there in the front of the room and call out the individual names like it was a high-school graduation. The technicians will be tired at that point in the day and a roll call is the *last* thing they'll want to put up with. All you'll accomplish will be to dull the sharp edge of that inspirational closing you just hit them with.

If you have a few bucks in the budget, consider an embroidered patch instead of a certificate. Companies that sell promotional products such as hats and tee shirts can design and produce great-looking, custom patches for you. These cost a couple of bucks each, but they look *terrific* on a work uniform and the technicians will think about you whenever they get dressed to go to work.

It's a nice touch.

Thank them again.

Thank you!

And in that same spirit of humility I want to thank *you* for taking the time to listen to me. I wish you well with *every* class you teach. I sincerely hope the technicians you encounter don't pelt you with pizza crust and beer cans. I hope crazed dogs and crows never visit your meeting rooms. I hope those same rooms never flood or burst into flames. I hope that *you* never burst into flames! May the good Lord protect you from gospel choirs and country/western music in the adjoining room. May all of your microphones work and all of your switches be wired properly.

I hope the towns to which you travel never pave their streets on the days you visit. I also hope they don't lock your stuff in their parking garage. I *sincerely* hope no nose ever gets punched while you're at the helm – even if might be an arrogant engineer's nose. May all the night clerks have keys and long extension cords. I pray that you'll never have to consider *why* they put those little stickers on the fruit, or have to wonder whether Delta Faucet advertised on last year's Super Bowl.

Most of all, I hope you *never* meet that stingy cook with the fatty roast beef, or have to sleep in the broom closet at the Holiday Inn in Glenwood Springs, Colorado, even though your name is on their marquee.

And if Ray Combs should somehow rise from the dead, I sincerely hope that he doesn't show up at your seminar. But if he does, I hope it happens when you're young and impressionable.

Good luck, my friend.

Break a tongue!